STUDIES IN
ANGLO-FRENCH HISTORY

STUDIES IN
ANGLO-FRENCH HISTORY
DURING THE EIGHTEENTH, NINETEENTH
AND TWENTIETH CENTURIES

Edited by

ALFRED COVILLE

AND

HAROLD TEMPERLEY

Essay Index Reprint Series

BOOKS FOR LIBRARIES PRESS
FREEPORT, NEW YORK

First Published 1935
First Reprinting in this Series 1967
Second Reprinting 1969

STANDARD BOOK NUMBER:
8369-0343-9

LIBRARY OF CONGRESS CATALOG CARD NUMBER:
67-23197

PRINTED IN THE UNITED STATES OF AMERICA

CONTENTS

CONTENTS

PREFACE

THE way in which these studies have been compiled by historical experts of two nations, and the common aims of the writers, are fully described by M. Alfred Coville in the pages which follow this preface. They are the product of historical conferences at London in 1933 and at Paris in 1934. It is only needful to mention here that Professor Michel Lhéritier, Dr G. P. Gooch and Mr E. L. Woodward took part in the discussions but did not contribute to this volume. At Paris in 1934 there was a medieval section in addition to a modern one. This was attended by M. Coville, Chairman of the French National Committee, MM. Ferdinand Lot, Petit-Dutaillis, G. Mollat, A. Fliche and R. Fawtier, Professors F. M. Powicke, now Chairman of the British National Committee, Hilda Johnstone, J. H. Baxter, E. F. Jacob, Dr C. W. Previté-Orton, Miss Helen M. Cam, Messrs R. R. Betts and J. N. L. Myres.

The aim of the two conferences was that historians of both countries should widen their outlook by mutual interchanges of opinion and by friendly discussion of related problems. There was a time within my own recollection when such interchange of views either did not exist or brought little profit. I remember one British historian, who criticized Napoleon's Continental system because it violated Free Trade, the recognized commercial policy of all countries. I remember several French ones, who explained England's missionary zeal in abolishing the Slave-Trade as due to the promptings of a sinister commercial interest. These studies will show that progress has been made since that date, and will justify the experiment of a prolonged and systematized exchange of historical views.

One of the best papers at the Conference of Paris was that of M. Picavet on the influence of England upon Marshal Turenne, followed by an interesting discussion. Since the author's recent and lamented death the manuscript has not been found. Otherwise all the papers in the modern sections are given, though some have been since modified by the authors in view of the discussions, or in the light of fresh material. In preparing them for the press I have owed much to the ripe judgment of M. Coville and to the indefatigable zeal of M. Renouvin in providing translations from the French. I do not wish to avoid the responsibility of editing, but I feel that they are entitled to the major share of any credit which the volume may gain among either scholars or general readers.

Nearly all of the papers deal directly with the interaction of France and England upon one another, in respect to institutions, policies, finance or diplomacy. The themes of English contributors are the aftermath of the Treaty of Utrecht; Stanhope, Carteret and Fleury; the day's work at the Foreign Office under Palmerston; two years of Eastern policy under Salisbury; Gambetta's approach to England. The French contributors in every case study both English and French aspects of the subject. M. Cahen subjects political terms, M. Hauser finance, and M. Halévy public opinion, to this double test. Three more modern contributors deal with more restricted fields and quote from newer materials. M. Pagés uses the unpublished papers of Persigny to illustrate the tortuous policy of Napoleon III, which resulted in the annexation of Savoy and in estrangement from England. M. Mantoux, with new documents from the French archives, dares to handle the Fashoda question and the *début* of M. Paul Cambon in London. M. Renouvin quotes from unpublished French documents and published British ones, in order to pass judgment on the naval and military conversations of the two General Staffs on the eve of the War. Thus subjects, which touch on national honour and good faith, have been discussed in amity by the historians of two countries. What better justification can be offered for these Anglo-French Conferences, or for these studies which are the fruit of them?

HAROLD TEMPERLEY

February 1935

AVANT-PROPOS

CE livre n'est pas seulement un recueil d'études originales sur les relations de l'Angleterre et de la France à l'époque moderne et contemporaine: par son origine, par les faits mêmes dont il reste le témoignage durable, il est un document historique.

Soit en politique, soit dans le domaine purement spirituel, on a beaucoup parlé et depuis longtemps d'entente cordiale, de coopération intellectuelle, de compréhension réciproque. Mais la politique est changeante et suit des voies sinueuses; la coopération intellectuelle, si elle ne se marque pas par des objets bien définis, risque de se perdre dans l'universalité; la compréhension réciproque ne se réalise vraiment que par des contacts immédiats. C'est ce contact immédiat que les Comités britannique et français des Sciences historiques ont voulu créer, organiser pour les recherches d'histoire intéressant les deux pays.

Ce n'est pas seulement en effet par l'action du présent ou la prévision toujours incertaine de l'avenir que les peuples peuvent se rapprocher, c'est aussi par la connaissance impartiale de leur passé. Combien fécond peut être à cet égard un travail non pas subordonné, mais coordonné avec sympathie et confiance. Et il ne s'agit pas seulement de rechercher comment et pourquoi dans le passé deux grands peuples se sont connus ou méconnus. Les questions de méthode, la poursuite d'un même idéal scientifique sont les liens les plus sûrs, les moyens les plus efficaces de s'entendre, de faire, en bon accord, du travail historique une création continue. Et à ce double point de vue, quel meilleur champ d'action que l'histoire si mouvementée, si fertile en enseignements de la France et de l'Angleterre? Ainsi les études historiques ne sont pas seulement la satisfaction d'un activité étroitement scientifique et nationale, ce qui d'ailleurs est déjà d'une haute noblesse: elles sont un des éléments essentiels de la conscience universelle; s'associer librement pour les harmoniser et les perfectionner, c'est travailler à la fois pour l'amitié, pour la vérité et pour la paix.

Ce sont ces pensées qui ont inspiré la première démarche du Comité français des Sciences historiques auprès du Comité britannique, en novembre 1932, lorsqu'il a proposé des rencontres et des échanges de travaux entre historiens anglais et français. Du côté anglais, on prit fort légitimement le temps nécessaire de la réflexion: une telle proposition devait être acceptée sans arrière pensée, sans objections ni défiance; il fallait aussi se rendre compte des conditions et des moyens de réalisation. A cet égard, l'esprit pratique des confrères anglais trouva l'occasion de se manifester heureusement. A la fin de 1933, le Président du Comité britannique, d'accord avec le Comité de l'Institut des recherches historiques de l'Université de Londres, présenta un projet très simple, d'exécution facile: une réunion sans apparat, mais franchement cordiale entre huit ou dix historiens de chaque côté, qui apporteraient les résultats de certaines de leurs recherches, de celles qui leur sembleraient le mieux capables d'intéresser la réunion, d'éveiller des discussions amicales, de déterminer quelques conclusions nouvelles. Ainsi furent présentées et discutées les études qui remplissent la première partie du présent volume. Aucun des Français invités à Londres n'oubliera le charme et le profit des trois séances tenues à l'Institut des recherches historiques, de leur confortable simplicité, des causeries spontanées qui s'y échangèrent. Pour commencer ces entretiens, les baraquements de l'Institut avaient je ne sais quoi d'approprié, comme lorsqu'on se met en ménage sans autre souci que le bonheur réciproque, en laissant à l'avenir le soin d'embellir l'installation première. Il est inutile d'insister sur les sujets qui furent traités, puisque l'objet de ce volume est d'en faire connaître le développement. On constatera qu'aucun sujet n'a paru pouvoir être considéré comme déplacé ou prématuré. Nos méthodes avaient les mêmes principes; les communications et les discussions donnèrent la preuve immédiate que les convictions scientifiques étaient égales de part et d'autre. Puis notre déjeuner à l'Université, nos visites à la Bibliothèque du Château de Windsor et au Collège d'Eton, la réception de la Royal Historical Society, le dîner au London School of Economics furent le prolongement naturel de notre réunion. Car partout, par la bonne grâce de leurs hôtes, les historiens français se sentirent vraiment *at home*.

A des entretiens aussi réussis, il fallait un lendemain; ce ne pouvait être qu'un commencement. Il fut décidé qu'en 1934 pareille réunion serait organisée à Paris par le Comité français. Elle a eu lieu en effet les 26 et 27 mars dernier. Les mêmes principes ont présidé à nos échanges. Nul aspect de cours ou de conférence, bien que le cadre fût la Sorbonne; la même cordialité, la même confiance, la même tenue historique, scientifique. Les historiens anglais avaient donné l'année précédente un trop bon exemple pour qu'il ne fût pas suivi. On trouvera dans la seconde partie de ce volume les communications présentées. Elles restèrent strictement fidèles au même esprit de sincérité et impartialité; elles apportèrent toutes des éléments nouveaux soit par la manifestation de documents inédits, soit par l'étude critique des documents déjà publiés. Toutes viennent s'insérer utilement dans le cadre de l'histoire générale des relations de la France et de l'Angleterre. Mais il est apparu de nouveau et plus fortement encore que ce n'est là qu'une partie du profit tiré de part et d'autre: se connaître, échanger des opinions, des indications précieuses de documents, parler des livres récents, se mettre au courant des travaux en cours, se confier ses projets pendant les heures libres, à déjeuner, tout en parcourant l'Île-de-France, tirer des suggestions même de visites comme celles à la Cathédrale de Chartres et au Château de Chantilly, quel progrès pour tous sur les habitudes anciennes d'isolement et d'ignorance réciproques! Quel élargissement d'horizon! Quelle conscience nouvelle tirée de tels rapprochements, qu'il s'agisse de l'un ou de l'autre pays! Se connaître surtout, c'est-à-dire savoir ce que l'on pense, confronter des opinions différentes, fraterniser—le mot n'est pas de trop—dans la pénétration des esprits, dans la liberté et le respect mutuels, dans la bienfaisante diversité. Cela, on l'a si bien senti que l'on n'a pas manqué de se donner rendez-vous pour l'an prochain en Angleterre. Et l'exemple a été contagieux, puisqu'à la réunion d'histoire moderne et contemporaine s'est jointe à Paris une réunion franco-anglaise d'histoire du Moyen-Age, qui, sauf la différence des époques étudiées, a ressemblé à la première comme une sœur.

Si l'œuvre ainsi commencée promet d'être aussi solide qu'utile, c'est parce qu'elle est libre de toute attache qui pourrait, avec les meilleures intentions du monde, en altérer le caractère. Vue avec bienveillance par les organisations qualifiées, par les universités, les Sociétés historiques, elle a sa seule raison d'être en elle-même. A cette liberté nous tenons comme à la seule garantie efficace de la valeur de nos travaux. Mais ne voulant pas garder pour nous seuls le profit des études présentées, il a été décidé, sur l'heureuse initiative des historiens anglais, de les mettre sous les yeux du public compétent. Il n'était que justice que la première édition fût une édition anglaise puisque c'est à Londres, dans la chaude hospitalité de Malet Street, que la tradition a été créée et que, pour prendre une expression familière, notre amitié historique a eu sa lune de miel.

A. COVILLE

Paris, 10 *juin* 1934

I

THE EIGHTEENTH CENTURY

1. The Anglo-French Alliance, 1716–31

by

SIR RICHARD LODGE

THE Anglo-French alliance, adjusted by Stanhope and Dubois in October 1716, and expanded into a Triple alliance by the adhesion of the Dutch in January 1717, is quite as deserving to be called a "diplomatic revolution" as the Austro-French alliance of 1756, to which the term is usually applied. In a sense the earlier alliance was the more revolutionary of the two because it was more sudden and unanticipated. It had its origin in the common dynastic interests of the houses of Hanover and Orleans, both of which demanded the maintenance of the Utrecht settlement, and it is a curious fact that, though the Orleans influence declined in France with the death of the Regent in 1723, the final collapse of the alliance was deferred until the uncertainty as to the succession in France was removed by the birth of the Dauphin in 1729.

The Utrecht settlement, including the whole series of treaties which closed the Spanish Succession War, left, as such settlements are wont to do, a number of sore places behind. The avowed malcontents, Austria and Spain, resented the partition of the Spanish dominions which the two rulers, Charles VI and Philip V, had claimed as their undivided inheritance, but each had additional grievances. Austria was indignant at the severance of Sicily from Naples and at the Barrier treaty, which in many ways curtailed Austrian sovereignty in the Low Countries. To Spain the retention of Gibraltar by England was a running sore, and the intrusion of England into her colonial trade was almost equally resented. France was conscious that the Utrecht

3

treaty was a fortunate escape from the threatened humiliation which had seemed inevitable in 1709 and 1710, and that sanguine hopes for the future might be based upon the seating of a Bourbon dynasty on the throne of Spain. On the other hand, French dignity had been insulted by the compulsory dismantling of Dunkirk and by the equally compulsory desertion of her Stuart guests, while she had no reason to welcome the exclusion of the Bourbons from Italy, or the Barrier deliberately erected against French aggression, or the territorial and commercial gains of England. Thus France must be reckoned among the malcontent powers, though exhaustion might make her for a time a passive malcontent. England, as the chief framer of the settlement, seemed to be the obvious champion of its maintenance, and Bolingbroke had taken very good care that English gains should be substantial. But even England had one bugbear. The Tory ministers, in defiance of Whig denunciations, had left a Bourbon on the throne of Spain. Even if adequate precautions had been taken, which was doubtful, against a future union of the French and Spanish kingdoms, there was every probability that the dynastic tie would, sooner or later, combine the two states in the pursuit of common aims, and that this would endanger both the European balance and the security of the Hanoverian dynasty in England. J. R. Seeley wrote an article for the first number of the *English Historical Review*, in which he contended that the later Family Compacts (in 1733, 1743 and 1761) fully justified the Whig condemnation of the treaty of Utrecht.

The Whig ministers who came into office on the accession of George I were perforce converted from critics into champions of the Utrecht treaty, because that treaty was, after the Act of Settlement, the strongest buttress of the Hanoverian succession. They had some

hopes of co-operation from France when Orleans became Regent, but those hopes disappeared when France
continued in the new reign to watch with obvious
sympathy the Jacobite movements in England and
Scotland. The ministers therefore had no alternative but
to follow the familiar Williamite tradition of antagonism
to France, and to seek the reconstruction of the Grand
alliance which their Tory predecessors had shattered.
Hence the Barrier treaty of 1715, which was designed to
link Austria with the Maritime Powers in permanent
hostility to France, and this was followed on 5 May 1716
by the conclusion of the treaty of Westminster with the
Emperor. The English ministers also sought, for obvious
reasons, to widen the split between France and Spain
which had developed since Louis XIV had betrayed his
willingness to abandon his grandson in 1709. Here also
they achieved some success. The proud Spanish nobles,
boastful that Philip V owed the retention of his crown
rather to Castilian loyalty than to French arms, were eager
to throw off the tutelage which had been tolerated only
so long as French support had been indispensable. And
when the regency fell to Orleans, whom Philip detested
as a rival for the French succession and also as a personal
enemy, the split between the two courts became a gulf.
This enabled the English envoy, George Bubb, to conclude two commercial treaties with Alberoni in December 1715 and April 1716. There were, however, two
snags in the way of the Whig policy. The Spanish Queen
and her minister intended by these mercantile concessions to purchase English connivance for their ambitious
designs in Italy. As such connivance would have involved a breach with Austria and a rupture of the
renascent Grand alliance, England could not earn the
purchase money, and without it the Bubb treaties were
not likely to be more than paper promises. Another

trouble was that the Emperor was turning his attention eastwards and was about to embark on another of those Turkish wars which had made Austria in the past such an unsatisfactory ally. At this juncture, in the autumn of 1716, when English prospects were rather murky, came those overtures from Dubois, which offered to convert France from an opponent into a supporter of the Utrecht settlement. Stanhope, in spite of his Whig prejudices, was quick to see the advantages of such a conversion, and hence arose the Triple alliance.

The most interesting, and from the English point of view the most successful, period of the Anglo-French alliance was from 1716 to 1720. In these years the co-operation of the two powers performed a double task. (1) It brought about that series of treaties which settled all the quarrels among the Baltic states, except that between Sweden and Russia in which Peter the Great would admit no mediation. (2) English diplomacy induced Charles VI to make peace with the Turks and to join France and England in what was called the Quadruple alliance. This combination crushed the Spanish attempt to make fundamental changes in the Utrecht settlement in Italy. The British fleet destroyed the nascent navy of Spain and a French army dismantled the fortresses and dockyards of Catalonia. Philip V had to dismiss Alberoni and to accept the terms of the Quadruple alliance, which had gratified the Emperor by allowing him to exchange Sardinia for Sicily. The bribe offered to Spain for its tardy adhesion was the recognition of the claim of Elizabeth Farnese's eldest son, Don Carlos, to succeed in Parma and Tuscany on the extinction of the male lines of the ruling dynasties. If Spain had yielded without fighting, Stanhope would have added Gibraltar to the bribe.

This apparent triumph was almost fatal to the Anglo-French alliance, and ushered in a period (1720–4) in which it was in danger of dissolution. Public opinion in France was outraged by the employment of French troops against the grandson of Louis XIV, in whose cause France had fought for so many years, and France seemed to be degraded by playing the part of a cat's-paw for England. Stanhope's death transferred the control of foreign policy to the less capable hands of Townshend, who had had no share in recent achievements. Orleans and Dubois began to turn in the direction of that close alliance with Spain which England dreaded, and hoped to conciliate Spain by obtaining for her the cession of Gibraltar. The new English ministers discovered the negotiation, and could only minimize its dangers by sharing in it. The result was that in 1721 the Franco-Spanish treaty of 27 March was expanded on 13 June into a new Triple alliance between France, England and Spain, which undertook to put pressure upon Austria to accept the Spanish interpretation of the terms upon which Don Carlos was to succeed to Parma and Tuscany. At the instigation of France George I wrote his famous letter to Philip V in which he undertook to seek parliamentary approval for the cession of Gibraltar. These agreements mark a curious change in the attitude and in the balance of the Anglo-French alliance. In 1718 England and France, already acting together, induced Austria to join in imposing terms upon Spain. In 1721 France and Spain, already allied together, accept English assistance in inducing Austria to accept terms demanded by Spain. In 1721 France is as clearly the predominant partner as England had been from 1718 to 1720. Matters became worse when later in the year Orleans and Dubois, in complete secrecy, arranged a double marriage alliance with the court of Madrid.

7

Louis XV was betrothed to the daughter of Philip V and Elizabeth Farnese, and Don Luis, the heir to the Spanish throne, was to marry a daughter of the Regent. The two prospective brides were exchanged on the frontier in January 1722, and later in that year there was yet another betrothal. Don Carlos was to marry a second daughter of Orleans, and she was to follow her sister to Spain. England, wholly unconsulted on these important matters, could only feign a pleasure which she did not feel. This apparent tightening of the Franco-Spanish alliance would probably have driven England to break away from France and to return to the traditional connection with Austria but for the friction caused by Charles VI's Ostend Company and for Hanoverian quarrels with the Emperor over affairs in Germany. The death of Orleans at the end of 1723 broke the dynastic tie which had brought England and France together in 1716, and the office of First Minister in France was transferred to the Duke of Bourbon, who had no quarrel with Philip V but rather the reverse. These changes seemed to bring France and Spain still closer together and thus increased the disquietude of England. The uneasiness of Anglo-French relations was reflected in the dilatory proceedings of the Congress of Cambray and in constant bickerings about the alleged failure of France to fulfil her promises with regard to Dunkirk. That the alliance survived 1724 was mainly due to the confusion in Europe caused by Philip V's dramatic abdication in January and his return to the throne some eight months later. During the interval the future attitude of Spain was so uncertain that deliberate diplomacy was almost impossible.

The year 1725 ushered in the third and final stage in the history of the Anglo-French alliance, and during the following six years it passed through sundry vicissitudes.

When Elizabeth Farnese resumed control in the autumn of 1724, she was so disgusted with the inadequate support given to Spain by the allies of 1721, that she sent Ripperda to Vienna to suggest a direct reconciliation with the Emperor, who had plenty of grievances of his own against England and France. It is unlikely that anything would have come of this strange negotiation, whose secrecy was very imperfect, if Bourbon had not chosen this inauspicious moment to repudiate the marriage contract of 1721, to send back the young Infanta to Spain, and to hunt for an adult bride for Louis XV. This insult so exasperated Philip V and Elizabeth that they broke off diplomatic relations with France, returned the two Orleans princesses, one widowed and one unmarried, and authorized Ripperda to conclude a treaty with Austria upon terms which hitherto Spain had rejected with scorn. Thus what had seemed impossible had actually happened, and the two irreconcilable claimants, who had fought so obstinately against each other over the Spanish Succession, had not only settled their quarrel without mediation, but had actually become close allies. The conclusion of the treaties at Vienna on 30 April 1725, and the suspicion that behind their ostensible terms were secret and perilous agreements, so alarmed Bourbon and Townshend that the Anglo-French alliance, so recently on the verge of collapse, was solemnly renewed by the treaty of Hanover on 3 September 1725. This treaty, in its turn, produced the very danger which it was intended to provide against, and on 5 November Austria and Spain concluded the secret treaty, whose previous existence had been assumed by the Hanover allies. By this treaty the Austro-Spanish alliance was to be cemented by a double marriage. The two sons of Elizabeth Farnese were to marry at some future date two of the Emperor's daughters. If this meant, as Elizabeth Farnese hoped and as Ripperda assured her, that Don Carlos was to marry the eldest archduchess, and if she should inherit her father's dominions, a situation would be created in Europe which was almost equally alarming to England and to France.

I have called the treaty of Hanover in 1725 a "renewal" of the Anglo-French alliance. It might with at least equal accuracy be described as a new alliance, as it was made under altered conditions and with quite different purposes. It is impossible in a short summary to describe its later history.[1] All that can be done is to call attention to the dates of certain events which directly affected the alliance, to note the chief diplomatic turning-points, and to estimate the main purposes of the protagonists in the diplomatic turmoil. There was a brief period in which a "state of war" existed between England and Spain, but the actual hostilities were of minute proportions, and the general conflagration in Europe, which at one time seemed inevitable, never broke out.

The three events which directly affected the relations between England and France are as follows. In June 1726 Bourbon ceased to be First Minister and Fleury took his place with greater authority than the Duke had ever held. In August 1727 Morville, who shared with Bourbon the responsibility for breaking off the Spanish marriage, was removed from the French Foreign Office, and Chauvelin, the Garde des Sceaux, succeeded him. On 3 September 1729 Maria Leczynska, the wife of Louis XV, gave birth to a daughter. Each of these events weakened the Anglo-French alliance,

[1] I have attempted to do this in a Presidential Address to the Royal Historical Society on "The Treaty of Seville, 1729", printed in the Society's *Transactions*, Fourth Series, vol. XVI.

and also weakened England as a partner in the alliance. As long as Bourbon was in office, circumstances, as they had done in Stanhope's day, gave a dominant influence to England. Bourbon was, in the eyes of Spain, the villain of the drama. It was his reckless conduct in sending back the Infanta without adequate explanation and apologies which had driven Spain into this alliance with France's secular enemy. Thus France under Bourbon's guidance had more need of England than England had of France.[1] The accession of Fleury to power altered the whole situation. He had done nothing to alienate Spain, and was believed to have condemned his predecessor's action, or at any rate his manner of doing it. As a loyal churchman, he was expected to repudiate the alliance with heretics. And as a good Frenchman, he could be trusted not to allow England to dictate the policy of France or to drag France once more into war against the Bourbon king whom France had placed on the Spanish throne. All these expectations were not actually fulfilled, but to a large extent they were justified. England was now the suppliant for the maintenance of the alliances, and Horace Walpole, Sir Robert's brother, claimed the credit of having gained Fleury's goodwill for England. Fleury judiciously let him exult in his success, but his goodwill went no further than the interests of France seemed to demand. The appointment of Chauvelin as Foreign Secretary was a deliberate move on Fleury's part towards Spain and away from England. It provided him with a convenient colleague upon whose shoulders he could lay the blame for any failure to conform to English wishes, and in this way he fooled the Walpoles for ten years. Finally, as

[1] Dubois said the same thing in defence of the terms of the alliance in 1716: "we needed their alliance, they did not need ours". See Baudrillart, *Philippe V et la Cour de France*, II, 464.

long as there was a prospect of a disputed succession in France, Fleury was not prepared to part company from England. The birth of the Dauphin enabled him to establish relations with Spain which rendered the English alliance, on the terms laid down in 1725, no longer a necessity for France.

The diplomatic time-table may be briefly stated. By the end of 1726 Spain and England had drifted into war with each other. A squadron under Hosier blockaded the Spanish treasure-fleet at Porto Bello, and Spain, in retaliation, opened trenches before Gibraltar and seized the "permitted ship" at Vera Cruz. Both belligerents appealed to their allies, and, if the appeal had been successful, the war would have become general. But there was a convenient dispute as to who was the aggressor, and Fleury had no intention of being dragged, as Orleans and Dubois had been dragged, into a war with Spain. As the Emperor was equally averse to the bellicose policy of Spain, it was easy for the two pacific powers to draft the preliminaries of peace, which were signed at Paris on 31 May 1727, and, as Spain had no representative at Paris, were signed again at Vienna on 11 June. In spite of the signature of the Spanish minister at Vienna, Elizabeth Farnese refused to give to these preliminaries an interpretation which England would accept. France undertook to mediate, and her ambassador adjusted terms with Spain on 3 December 1727. Again England rejected this agreement and forced Fleury to cancel it, and it was not till 6 March 1728 that a Convention signed at the Pardo finally put an end to the Anglo-Spanish war. As agreed in the Convention, the settlement of outstanding disputes was remitted to a Congress which was opened at Soissons on 14 June 1728, but the actual negotiations were speedily transferred to the French court, where they could be guided by Fleury and Chauvelin. These negotiations failed to produce a general treaty, but they did result in a separate treaty, adjusted in Paris but signed at Seville on 9 November 1729, between Spain on one side and the Hanover allies on the other. This left the Emperor isolated, and he did not give way till 1731, when he concluded with England the treaty of Vienna, whose subsequent acceptance by Spain settled most of the complicated problems which had agitated Europe for the last twelve years.

The major protagonists in the diplomatic drama were Elizabeth Farnese and Cardinal Fleury: while comparatively minor parts were played until 1729 by the Emperor Charles VI and by England, as represented by Lord Townshend, the Principal Secretary of State in England until 1729. After 1729 both England, now guided by Walpole, and the Emperor emerged into far greater prominence. English interests were fairly simple. The maintenance of the Protestant succession and of the balance of power impelled resistance to any marriage project which might bring the Austrian dominions to a Bourbon prince. It would be intolerable that the Bourbons should rule in Vienna as well as in Paris and Madrid. Public opinion in England demanded, in addition, the dissolution of the Ostend Company, together with the retention of Gibraltar and of the mercantile concessions extorted from Spain. The French alliance, not popular in itself, would be maintained as long as it served for these ends.

Charles VI had welcomed the Spanish alliance because he wanted money, naval support for his Ostend Company, and recognition by a great power of the Pragmatic Sanction which was to secure the undivided succession to his heiress, if he should leave no son. But he had no desire to pay even the moderate price which had been stipulated, and still less the price which the Spanish Queen persistently demanded. He had no such love for the Spanish Bourbons as to marry his heiress to one of them, and he knew that such a marriage would endanger rather than secure the unity of his dominions. And he was as reluctant as ever to admit a Bourbon to the Italian duchies, which would provide an irresistible temptation to steal as much as possible of those Italian provinces which had been detached from Spain.

Elizabeth Farnese was more than ever the dictator of Spain after she had induced her husband to resume his crown. She was an Italian, and had none of Philip's affection for France. The Austrian alliance was peculiarly her work and she clung to it with the tenacity of a creator. She was dazzled by the prospect of raising her beloved son to be ruler of the Austrian dominions and possibly Holy Roman Emperor. It was this, besides her own temper, which made her so bellicose. She knew Charles VI's reluctance to promise to Don Carlos the hand of Maria Theresa, but she trusted that war would make the Emperor so dependent upon Spain that he would be forced to give way. She was, however, sufficiently practical to realize that her grandiose scheme might fail, and she never lost sight of her original purpose, the endowment of her son with as ample an Italian principality as possible, and the retention in the hands of her descendants of the duchies of Parma and Tuscany, which they could claim through herself. Finally, she knew that she was a foreigner in Spain, that she must conciliate Spanish pride, and this made her press the demand for Gibraltar, and contend that England must pay for the retention of the *Asiento* by the surrender of the fortress. But the event proved that, when she was forced to make a choice, the interests of her family easily outweighed those of Spain.

The dominant figure, however, from 1726 to 1729 was undoubtedly Cardinal Fleury. His tortuous methods cannot blind us to the simplicity of his aims. In his eyes the enemy of France was still the house of Habsburg. His supreme purpose was to detach the Bourbon dynasty in Spain from its unnatural alliance with Austria. Spain must not only return to alliance with France, but also to that docile alliance which had existed in the days of Louis XIV and the Princess Orsini. As long as Elizabeth Farnese clung to her marriage project for Don Carlos, so long Fleury must cling to his alliance with England. He had no intention of going to war with Spain as France had done in 1719, but he must threaten such war as a means of coercing the Spanish Queen. But in the alliance with England France must be the leader, and as long as he had to deal with Townshend he kept the upper hand. Fleury's supreme diplomatic triumph at this period, only achieved after many disappointments, was the conclusion of the treaty of Seville. He had not only detached Spain from Austria and bound Spain once more to France, but he had also, as he thought, averted the danger of a renewal of the Grand alliance by making both England and Holland parties to what was essentially a Bourbon alliance.

But the very completeness of Fleury's triumph in 1729 involved certain very obvious dangers. The pacification of Europe demanded that Austria must be somehow induced to accept the terms prescribed for her by the Seville treaty, just as Spain in 1719 had to be induced to accept the terms laid down in the Quadruple alliance. Spain had then yielded only to superior force, and Elizabeth Farnese clamoured in 1730 that Austria must be subjected to the same armed coercion. If England had become a partner of the two Bourbon courts in a war against her former ally, she would suffer the same humiliation as Stanhope had imposed upon France in 1719. If Townshend had remained as the dominant Secretary of State, his exasperation at Charles VI's obstinacy might have led him into a fatal blunder. But Townshend's colleagues were no longer disposed to follow his guidance or to submit to Bourbon dictation. Sir Robert Walpole substituted for his brother-in-law a more submissive Secretary of State in the person of Lord Harrington, and took the control of foreign policy into his own hands. In spite of the clause of the treaty of Hanover which forbade separate negotiations on the part of the allied powers, secret overtures were made to Austria. The Emperor was offered the irresistible bribe of a guarantee of the Pragmatic Sanction by the Maritime Powers. In return for this Charles VI was to annul his charter to the Ostend Company and to accept, with regard to the Italian duchies, the terms laid down in the treaty of Seville. The treaty of Vienna pacified Europe, but the Bourbon powers had no active share in the pacification.

The treaty of Vienna, and still more the way in which it was negotiated, dealt a death-blow to the Anglo-French alliance. Fleury never forgot or forgave the way in which France had been suddenly jockeyed out of her leading position in Europe. At any moment during the last five years he could have detached Charles VI from his alliance with Spain by acceptance of the Pragmatic Sanction. But he had deliberately refused to pay this price because France had no interest in securing the Austrian dominions from partition. And now England had stepped in, and, without any consultation with France, had given the guarantee which France had notoriously condemned. And the injury went deeper still. Fleury had brought Spain back to France, but he was now confronted once more by the dreaded spectre of the Grand alliance. It is to Fleury's credit that he averted an immediate rupture by concealing his chagrin and by professing his continued good will to the two Walpole brothers. This enabled him before many years had passed to pay them back in their own coin. There are few more interesting stories in diplomatic history than that of Fleury's tit-for-tat—how he and Chauvelin picked a quarrel with Austria on the convenient pretext of the Polish Succession, which was no concern of England; how they lulled the Dutch into a premature pledge of neutrality; how Fleury fooled the Walpoles by professing to consult them about the terms of a settlement, and then made it without their intervention; and finally, how France, after endless professions of disinterestedness, emerged from the war with an assured reversion of Lorraine. But the story has been told at length by Professor Vaucher, and it is more appropriate to a narrative of Anglo-French dissension than to that of the alliance between the two states.

It is clear from the sketch which I have drawn in preceding pages that the Anglo-French alliance, even in the years when it was a real force, was always rather fragile, that it had its origin in dynastic rather than in national interests, and that it was never popular in either country. The two powers were harnessed together as a tandem rather than as a pair, and there was a constant competition as to which should be the leader. Yet, in spite of its defects, the alliance had important results. It preserved the Utrecht settlement practically intact for twenty years, and it averted all but very slight infractions of European peace. With its dissolution came the break-down of the great settlement, and the successive wars of the Polish and Austrian Successions and the Seven Years' War. This may be held to suggest that a dominant alliance of great powers, especially when faced by disturbing forces which are not united, is a better guarantee of peace than an uneasy and fluctuating balance between two equal and competing groups. But a good deal depends upon the motives which guide the dominant alliance. Some of the apparent merits of the Anglo-French alliance from 1716 to 1731 must be attributed to the men who played the most prominent parts in its history, to Stanhope and Dubois (an able statesman if a bad man), and to Fleury and Walpole.

2. A short Comparison between the Secretaries of State in France and in England during the Eighteenth Century

by

BASIL WILLIAMS

I N both England and France the Secretaries of State, as they became, were originally simply personal secretaries of the King, their duty being to transmit the King's orders, to write letters on his instructions to foreign potentates and to the royal officials at home and abroad. Thus at first they had no personal responsibility, as long as they faithfully sent out the King's orders and wrote his letters as he directed. As the royal business increased, the number of his secretaries increased correspondingly: it then became convenient to assign to each of these secretaries a special department of the royal business, to which he usually confined himself; but in the absence of one of his colleagues he might at any time be called upon to write the letters or send out the orders relating to another secretary's department. This development, quite natural when the King was the sole originator of policy, accounts for the curious distribution of functions, which was apt to cause difficulties when the King's secretaries had become Secretaries of State and to assume more or less personal responsibility for their actions and advice, either to the King or to Parliament. By the eighteenth century, when the departments had become stereotyped, these difficulties were very apparent.

In France there were three Secretaries of State in the eighteenth century: for Foreign Affairs, for War and for Marine; and in that respect their functions were clear and well defined; each of them could feel himself master, under the King, for one of these important departments. But in domestic affairs there was more confusion, for, as a relic, presumably, of the old non-responsible period, the affairs of the provinces of France were distributed, more or less at haphazard, between these three secretaries and also the Controller of Finances; hence there was no single person except the King, or Fleury during his virtual prime ministership, for internal policy. During such periods, especially during Louis XIV's reign, any difficulties were largely overcome by the King's own control and the advice of his well-equipped Councils.

Above all, as compared with England, France was fortunate in having only one foreign minister, who could take within his purview the whole of European politics and conduct French policy on consistent lines. Thus capable foreign ministers, such as Choiseul and Vergennes, had an initial advantage over their English colleagues. It is true that this excellent arrangement was occasionally interfered with during the century. The Regent, apparently in the belief that he would retain more power by dispensing with a single foreign minister, tried a conciliar system[1] under the chairmanship of an incompetent marshal, Huxelles, but he soon had to abandon the experiment and make Dubois entirely responsible to him for foreign affairs. Under Fleury Chauvelin for a time was nominally foreign minister; but the envoys of foreign powers, notably Horace Walpole and Waldegrave, got into the way of appealing from Chauvelin to Fleury, which was confusing to them, but in some respects served the purposes of the wily old cardinal well enough. Lastly, Louis XV had a private

---

[1] Known as the *Polysynodie, v. infra,* p. 33 n. 1.

foreign policy of his own, different from that of some of his foreign secretaries; but, being too lazy or unable to control his ministers, had a set of private envoys of his own, whose business it was to counteract the official policy expounded by the regular French ambassadors. A good system was, therefore, largely at the mercy of the King or Regent who was for the time being supreme.

But in spite of these aberrations, owing perhaps to a more effective tradition of royal control and the regular system, introduced by Richelieu and continued by some of his admirable successors, the French methods of foreign policy and office organization were far superior to those of England in this century.

(1) First and above all there was a fixed standard of foreign policy in the *raison d'état*, formulated indeed by Richelieu, but dating from long before his time, a standard by which the best policy to pursue on particular occasions could be decided. Of course too rigid a system has its dangers in the constantly varying circumstances of world affairs (France's early policy to Russia is a case in point); but, especially with weak foreign ministers, it is always useful to have a fixed principle as a guide.

(2) As a result partly of this guiding principle, the Instructions drawn up by the ministers to envoys on taking up their mission are clear and comprehensive, so that they had no excuse for not being able to determine on their line of action in almost any circumstance that might arise. These general Instructions were, of course, supplemented by directions on any question of import-ance that might arise on points of detail; and, to judge from Jusserand's remarks in his *Instructions, Angleterre*, the informal exchange of letters between envoys and minister or even the King in the time of Louis XIV greatly eased the smooth working of French diplomacy.

(3) The return of all diplomatic documents and their preservation in the archives of the ministry, which at any rate from the time of Mazarin became a fixed rule, must have greatly facilitated the intelligent appreciation of foreign conditions by ministers responsible for French foreign policy. Even to-day historians have cause to be grateful for this care in preserving diplomatic documents, carefully catalogued and indexed, as it greatly facilitates their task of research. The same applies even more to the great series of *Instructions aux Ambassadeurs* so nobly set forth in the *Recueil* published by the French government.

(4) Diplomacy in France, as was the case in few other countries of the eighteenth century, was a career often followed by successive members of the same family, notably the Colberts, a career for which there was definite training. This also helped to give that consistency and skill in foreign policy so remarkable during the whole reign of Louis XIV and not entirely absent from the less glorious days of his successor.

In England the traces of the domestic and purely personal origin of the two Secretaries of State lasted almost to the end of the eighteenth century. Thus, in addition to their clerkly salary of £100, they were still entitled, for their sustenance, to the right of receiving a certain allowance of dishes from the royal table, though this right was in practice commuted for a handsome monetary allowance, then with fees and allowances their income was made up to a considerable sum. Again, although in some departments of state a civil service was already in existence, the Secretaries of State, being still officially the King's scribes, were expected to write his letters and issue his orders as best they could, and to provide their own helpers. They had no official subordinates with a fixed tenure, and supplied their office needs with clerks and assistants personally appointed by themselves and liable to dismissal with a change of Secretary. Such a system naturally did not make for such continuity of policy as comes from a permanent staff to carry on the office traditions.

But the worst feature of the English system during most of the eighteenth century was that there was no Foreign Secretary as such, for the two Secretaries' duties were divided in the most haphazard fashion. In foreign affairs the Northern Secretary dealt with the Empire, Germany, Holland and the Baltic countries, while his colleague for the South dealt with the rest of Europe. Nor did their duties end there. They both carried out the present duties of the Home Secretary with no apparent system for the division of this work; both also, but chiefly the Southern Secretary, dealt with the colonies, except between 1768 and 1782, when there was a colonial Secretary; the Southern also dealt with Ireland. Scotland had a Secretary of its own in the years 1709–15, 1716–25 and 1742–6, but generally its affairs fell to the Northern and Southern departments indifferently. All orders to the admiralty, the military departments and the Committee on Trade and Plantations were issued by one of them indifferently. A further complication arose during the frequent absences of the first two Georges in Hanover. The King was always accompanied by one, and on one occasion by both Secretaries: then the Secretary with the King practically did the work of both offices, leaving to the colleague or substitute at home little to do except to transmit despatches and receive the orders sent from Hanover.

It is extraordinary that such a complicated and confused system did not create even more difficulties than it did. For example, our dealings with the Emperor and the Turk were chiefly concerned with the relations

between those two potentates, and yet the affairs of the
Turk were dealt with by one Secretary, those of the
Emperor by the other; similarly, during George I's
reign our relations with Russia depended largely on the
attitude of France, yet here again two Secretaries dealt
separately with those two countries. Again, it will be
observed that during the critical period of the 1715
rebellion there was no Secretary for Scotland, where
military operations were taking place, with the result
that orders were indifferently sent to the general in the
field by Townshend or Stanhope, then Secretaries of
State, and there is even one letter written by Townshend
with a postscript added by Stanhope. The difficulty of
securing the intimate co-operation between the two
Secretaries, so necessary for a reasonably consistent
policy, is well illustrated during the long tenure of office
by the Duke of Newcastle. A politician of mediocre
ability, but nevertheless consumed by a belief in his own
importance, he was habitually jealous of any colleague
with superior ability and power of initiative; in such cases
his method was to be constantly nagging at his brother-
Secretary and interfering with his province, with the
result that the colleague either resigned in disgust or was
dismissed by means of Newcastle's persistent intrigues.
Thus, in succession, Carteret, Harrington, Chesterfield,
Bedford and Sandwich were got rid of, until Newcastle
finally obtained in Holderness a colleague who was
"so good-natured you may tell him his faults and he will
mend them, and no pride in him, though a d'Arcy".

This absurd system was, however, mitigated during
some of the most important periods of the century by the
presence of a man of strong character in the ministry who
practically dictated the foreign policy of the nation.
During most of Stanhope's time he took sole responsibility for the conduct of both departments, Methuen and

Craggs being little more than his clerks; Walpole, though not Secretary, was dictator of foreign policy during most of his ministry; from 1742 to 1744 Carteret contemptuously left little for Newcastle to do, except to intrigue against him, though even he eventually succumbed to the Duke's intrigues. Finally, however, Pitt, when Secretary, took care that his pliant colleague Holderness should follow him implicitly and snapped his fingers at his nominal superior Newcastle: in fact Pitt had no scruple in interfering with Holderness's province and blasting with his indignation one of Holderness's subordinates who had dared to indulge in "dapplings for peace" without his leave. When George III came to the throne he attempted, with singular ill-success, to imitate Louis XIV and make his ministers, including the Secretaries, mere clerks to carry out his policy. But this system did not survive the loss of America; and in 1782 the sensible system was at last introduced of making one Secretary solely responsible for home affairs and another for all foreign affairs and for nothing else.

In another important respect the English system was inferior to the French in having no such clearly defined principles of foreign policy. It is true Newcastle was always trotting out his shibboleth of the "Old System" of alliances, and made a sorry mess of it between 1748 and 1756. But until Pitt came, it would almost be true to say, there was no real appreciation of what should be the objects of foreign policy or at any rate of the best means to carry them out. One result of this lack of logical precision is to be seen in the jejuneness of the formal Instructions to envoys abroad, especially as contrasted with the expositions of national policy conveyed in the French Instructions. Our Historical Society has recently followed the French example of publishing the official Instructions; but in order to do this effectively it has been constrained to neglect almost entirely the formal Instructions, which rarely contain anything but directions about ceremonial, and piece out the policy to different nations by the fuller despatches sent as occasion arose to the different capitals. Nor was it so easy for our Secretaries to gain an insight into the history of previous dealings, since their predecessors had often regarded many of the official records during their tenure of office as their perquisites and carried them off to bury them in their country mansions. Fortunately many of these records have been recovered and are now available, chiefly in the British Museum, instead of the Record Office, where they properly belong, such as the Carteret and Newcastle papers, the latter a priceless mine for eighteenth-century diplomatic and domestic affairs: others, such as Lord Lansdowne's, have gone to America.

No period, perhaps, illustrates so well the defects of both English and French methods of diplomacy in the eighteenth century as that between 1740 and 1756. As early as 1715 Louis, as shown in his instruction to St Luc, had realized that the old *raison d'état* of inveterate hostility to the Habsburgs needed revising, now that one frontier seemed safe by their expulsion from Spain, where a Bourbon prince was reigning, and the Austrian Habsburgs were chiefly preoccupied with the Turks. Accordingly he had instructed his ambassador to pave the way for an understanding with the Emperor. The unexpected alliance of the Emperor with the Bourbons of Spain in 1725 had for a time interrupted the co-operation with him begun by the Quadruple alliance; and the Polish War directed chiefly against him, though

futile as regards the Polish Succession, had at any rate
secured Lorraine, which gave France a secure frontier
on the Rhine. But in 1740, when France once more took
sides against the Habsburgs, she had nothing to gain
and much to lose. Her honour was smirched by the
breach of so recent a treaty, in which she had guaranteed
the Pragmatic Sanction in return for Lorraine and other
advantages; and, on a long view, she backed the wrong
horse in the rising power of Prussia, destined to take the
place of the Austrian monarchy as her most formidable
antagonist in the East. In this instance it was not so
much the French foreign office that was at fault as the
weakness of the minister Fleury. At the outset he opposed
the bellicose views of Belle-isle and the hotheads, who
thought the time had come to crush the Habsburg
power irretrievably, and gained the ear of the King
anxious only to assert himself but constitutionally unable to follow up a consistent line of his own. After the
Peace of Aix-la-Chapelle, which left everything undecided, the official French foreign policy under a set of
incompetent foreign ministers was allowed to drift.
Louis XV himself, under the influence of Mme de
Pompadour, reverted to the idea of his great-grandfather
in 1715, and listened favourably to the pertinacious
suggestions of Kaunitz for an alliance between the
secular enemies. Mme de Pompadour, indeed, seems to
have realized more clearly than anyone at Versailles
that the approaching struggle would be with England,
a struggle not chiefly on continental issues but for
dominion overseas; and that for France to be also waging
a continental war with the Austrians would merely be
playing into England's hands. But even so Louis had not
the courage to take the plunge soon enough. He listened
to the Austrians, but would not break away from his
uncertain ally and their implacable foe till the last

moment, when he was forced to do so by Frederick's conclusion of the treaty of Westminster and his insult to the haughty French ambassador Nivernois, Duc et Pair de France. Then, friendless in Europe, Louis at the last moment had to patch up a treaty with Vienna, which gave the Austrians the French support against Frederick that they needed, without entailing on them any corresponding obligations in return. Thus France, at the outset of the Seven Years' War, was left unaided to face the might of England and also to wage war against Frederick. In France, therefore, it was not so much a want of clear vision of the proper policy that was the cause of mistakes, as the weakness or indecision of those from time to time responsible for carrying out that policy.

In England during the years 1740–56 it is hard to find any guiding principle in policy. Walpole, it is true, and his successors had the honesty to admit that they were bound to help Maria Theresa in the War of the Austrian Succession. But beyond this there was little agreement. Carteret, at any rate, during his meteoric term of office from 1742 to 1744, at least knew what he wanted, but his indifference to the views and contempt for the capacity of his colleagues made it impossible for him to establish a definite system or even to remain in office against their opposition to his dictatorial personality. While staunch on the rights of Maria Theresa, he, alone at first, recognized that for England the main interest was to combat the French danger; and to unite all Germany as well as Savoy in alliance with England against France was his chief object. Had he been allowed by his jealous colleagues to do so as completely as he wished he might possibly, even without Frederick's aid, have delivered a crushing blow against France. But even he was blind to two elements in the problem: first, that Frederick was not at all interested in playing

England's game against France, being chiefly concerned in freeing Germany from all foreign interference after he had used France as his catspaw for abasing Maria Theresa: secondly, Carteret was not at all interested in the real issue between England and France, for colonial and maritime dominion, and could not conceive of any battle-ground between the two countries outside the continent of Europe. But at least Carteret had a clear, if limited, vision of England's policy: Newcastle, who directed England's foreign policy for the remaining years of the period, 1744–56, had merely a chaotic and indecisive mind, with no conception of foreign policy as a whole, unless his parrot-cry of maintaining the "Old System" of alliance between England, Holland and the Austrians can be called a policy. Until the peace of Aix-la-Chapelle he carried on the war on very much the same lines as he had objected to in Carteret, but in more halting fashion; and even Carteret, unsound as he was on extra-European interests, would not, as Newcastle did, have lamented the New Englanders' capture of Louisburg as likely to cause difficulties at the peace. During the eight preparatory years to 1756 Newcastle's only conception of plans for the renewal of the war that even he foresaw to be imminent, was to make feverish and fitful attempts at concluding onerous subsidy treaties with German princelings, whose contributions of men would at best be negligible in a continental war and utterly useless for the real struggle overseas. Quantity indeed rather than quality was his ideal for alliances, to such an extent that his last pair of alliances absolutely neutralized one another. For after engaging Elizabeth of Russia at great expense to keep a body of troops on her borders to invade the Empire in case of disturbance— which was most likely to come from Frederick of Prussia—he shortly afterwards made the treaty of West-

minster with the same Frederick, one of the main provisions of which was to prevent any foreign troops (such
as the Russians) from moving a step into Germany. The
outbreak of the war found him quite unprepared and
ready to find any scapegoat such as Byng to cover his
own negligence. Fortunately England then found a man
in Pitt, who could not only conceive of the objects of the
war as a whole and make deliberate plans to attain them,
but could fire the country, the colonies and the fighting
forces to enter into his views with understanding and
carry them out with enthusiasm. Perhaps Pitt's greatest
contribution to victory in the Seven Years' War may
even have been his clear enunciation of the aims of the
war and of the main lines whereby they could be secured.
But Pitt was an exception, not imitated by his successors
till we come to Castlereagh and Canning in a comprehensive plan of foreign policy. It is fortunate for this
country that at times of crisis such men have been apt to
emerge, for even up to these days, to judge from our
halting policy before the late war, our foreign office has
rarely been able to conceive of a fixed *raison d'état* which
can be put forward and prepare the country intelligently
for its responsibilities in peace or war.

3. The Prime Minister in France and England during the Eighteenth Century

by

LÉON CAHEN

NATURE and life have set up such a solidarity between our two countries that we can hardly,
either of us, understand and elucidate our own
history without referring to the other for certain elements
necessary to such comprehension. Furthermore, as the
influence of France and England has radiated throughout the world and often given a lead to universal life,
there are few general questions that can be solved without active investigations conducted jointly by the
historians of both countries. So true is this that when
the organising committee of the Warsaw Congress
included in their agenda the study of the movement of
thought in Europe during the eighteenth century, it set
the problem as being that of Franco-British influence on
the Continent; and indeed, failing that collaboration, a
complete and precise report on the subject would be out
of the question. But without stopping to explore such
wide avenues, it is easy to show by a few specific
examples how important has been the mutual influence
of our two nations, and how imperfectly understood or
imperfectly known that influence still remains. I shall
not venture into the field of diplomacy, since we have
among us here two specialists, who are recognized authorities—Sir Richard Lodge, whose mastery has at once
been attested by his recent edition of the Keene papers;
and our friend, Professor Vaucher, who has so entirely
revised the old judgments passed upon the policy of
Walpole and Fleury.

At the beginning of the nineteenth century, England had a Prime Minister as her official chief, and this institution, which so characteristically dominates the modern parliamentary life of many countries, has been looked upon by many observers as an admirable British invention. Yet its beginnings appear very obscure. No doubt some scholars have brought to light documents dating from the end of the seventeenth century, and showing that a few outstanding figures have been described in these or similar words. Interesting as these discoveries may be in the eyes of a scholar, they are not, to my mind, based on any solid and reliable foundation. The essential feature of these discoveries is a lack of continuity; the expression "prime minister" is not adhered to; it has no official, no specific character; it is a convenient way of describing, or estimating, the status of a man in office. There is nothing to support the inference that a regular tradition had been set up, much less that a constitutional organism had been created. The attention of an informed *élite* has been turned to these problems and there is a tendency to apply to contemporary matters words obviously borrowed from another age.

When Walpole took over his duties and consolidated his position more and more, he acquired so outstanding an authority that he acted like a viceroy. His brother Horace can say of him that he is "just like a Prime Minister".[1] But this is just because on the other side of the Channel there *is* a Prime Minister deriving his title from his

---

[1] The phrase was not only French in origin but there is some evidence to show that it was used in the sense of "sole minister" or Grand Vizier. Clarendon in 1661 declined to enjoy a pension out of the Exchequer "Under no other title but of being first Minister, a title so newly translated out of French into English, that it was not understood enough to be liked and every man would detest it for the burden it was attended with". *v.* Clarendon, *Autobiography*, I, 420 and Anson, *Law and Custom of the Constitution* [1896], II, 123 and n.

office, and Horace Walpole knows better than any other the importance of that office in the affairs of France and Europe.

France was not the only country to have Prime Ministers, but what happened in this realm left a deeper impression upon the English people than similar happenings in Spain or Italy. And the periods of revival in France, both in the seventeenth and in the eighteenth centuries, coincided with a signal concentration of authority in the hands not of a monarch, but of an exalted servant of the Crown; revival was the word I used, not power. Reference to contemporary documents suffices to show that both the Royalists and their opponents put their hopes or their fears in Richelieu, and afterwards in Mazarin. Louis XIV suppressed the practice for the time being, and when he died, the Régence seemed to usher in a period of anarchy. But after the chaos of the *polysynodie* (or system of substituting a council for each individual minister[1]) a return was made to the old tradition, not so much through the ambition of those who stood to gain by it, as by reason of the necessities of government. Dubois became Secretary of State for Foreign Affairs, then Cardinal Archbishop, and Prime Minister. This exaltation coincided with the attenuation of the quarrels of the Churches and of the nobility, and an accretion of prestige and power such as disquieted the English leaders.

After the death of Dubois, his work was very soon in jeopardy. The kingdom was threatened both by a war abroad and disorder at home. But Fleury assumed control of affairs; his status was higher than that of any of his predecessors, and the King had expressed his full trust in him. Within a few short months peace was restored both at home and abroad; financial balance was in sight and economic activity revived. Many

---

[1] Cp. *supra*, p. 20, n. 1.

Frenchmen attempted to belittle the Cardinal in the eyes of posterity—noblemen thirsting for wars and favours, philosophers or "Gallicans" hostile to the man who enforced the *Unigenitus* Bull, and reduced protesters to a respectful silence. Abroad, however, a different view has been taken, as witness, for instance, the evidence recently brought forward by our Swiss colleague, M. Corbaz. It would be easy, moreover, to find corroboration of that evidence in other documents, in statements made by Horace Walpole or Frederick the Great. In the eyes of all these observers, Fleury stands out as the saviour of a country in danger of becoming a second Poland, had he not been there as Prime Minister to put discords and ambitions under restraint. This was one of the reasons that impelled the enemies of France to intrigue against the Cardinal and sometimes to set Chauvelin above him.

That the English were particularly concerned at this state of things is but natural. A fear of France—not always unmixed with admiration—became an obsession with them. An ever more powerful current of opinion urged their rulers to take up the age-long struggle once more and carry it to the bitter end; to cancel the provisions of the treaty of Utrecht. But with a view to this struggle, which threatened to be a particularly dangerous one, it was necessary to infuse new life into the public services, to remedy current abuses, to adjust dissensions. Conditions, moreover, in the two countries were not without affording profound analogies. On our side, a youthful Monarch, obviously unequal to a task for the accomplishment of which he was totally unfitted, and of whom his subjects only asked for freedom to live and procreate; on your side a German ruler, less apathetic, less indifferent to insular affairs, not so incompetent, moreover, as he has often been made out to be, but impregnated, surrounded with Germanic influences and ambitions. Walpole's thirst for authority here unites with that of Bolingbroke. What is the "Patriot King" but a ruler who delegates his power to those who interpret the will of the nation?

All human affairs need a suitable environment. If the office of Prime Minister has become the keystone of the executive system, it is because it meets a national requirement. But the date, the appellation itself, un-British as it then was, points to the historical importance of the French example.

Furthermore, our country has experienced a change of method. A change of method and outlook, rather than of ideas. I would refer such as have any doubt on the point to Renouvin's book on the Provincial Assemblies. They will see there how the promoters of the system mean to restrict the new organisms to purely administrative functions, while begging the ministers to keep for themselves all that is essentially of a political and governmental character. They have no desire to weaken the power of the state, which they look upon as a vital guarantee of national unity, a conception which, in the case of the Jacobins, practically becomes a dogma. But after 1756, disasters and scandals discredited the Monarch. Louis XV reposed no trust in his ministers, whom he sometimes opposed. And even were he to have found a man to his liking, his favour would have made the recipient an object of suspicion and hatred. Public opinion would have viewed a concentration of power in one man as fraught with possibilities of abuse and tyranny. Louis XVI never really supported any one, and even if he had wished to do so, the increasing anarchy would have thwarted the action of a Prime Minister. Above all, the leaders pinned their hopes to the intervention of the nation at large: they subordinated the political to the legislative element. And, to them, uniformity of legislation appeared to be the real goal to be achieved. The organization of the executive power and the sovereignty of ministers were considered as minor points by the members of the Constituent Assembly, for what they were rather concerned with was to whittle down, not to consolidate the authority of the King. The office of Prime Minister was therefore revived, in France, but much later; not till about 1830, a full century after Fleury and Walpole, was it given an effective constitutional value, and the word applied to the function is, after all, much more akin to a British title than to the older French designation.

But if on that occasion—as well as on a few others which I have no time to specify—your country borrowed from ours, we have fully returned the compliment, and the influence exercised by Great Britain over the thought, manners and science of the eighteenth century is so much a matter of common knowledge, that it would seem needless to proclaim the fact. I am of opinion, however, that there are yet many gaps in our knowledge, and that more specific and more minute investigations would be required in order to put the finishing touches to it. We frequently lack certain documents that would help us to an exact comprehension of contemporary French political life and the evolution of our institutions, and of our customs and manners. Of these documents, the Revolution destroyed a number of vital ones, such as the records of the Paris Administration; some families jealously withhold papers which excite our curiosity. It often happens, too, that our sources are misleading, because they emanate from insincere or injudicious people. The *Memoirs* of Count de Bernis, for instance, have distorted our views as to the diplomacy of the Hundred Years' War.

In England, on the contrary, you have records that nothing has interfered with. Among these, there cannot fail to be a number of memoirs, letters, tales of travel in France, unpublished as yet, emanating from realists who were shrewd observers, from first-rate journalists of the old school, the fore-runners of the modern reporters, such as Arthur Young, whose works, edited in masterly fashion by M. Henri Sée, afford the best picture of the Old Régime at its close, or such writers even as Lord Chesterfield or Horace Walpole. By seeking out such documents, by publishing them, or by revealing them to us, at least, you would be doing us a signal service.

Another reason why we perceive but imperfectly the influence of England on French matters is that that influence was conditioned by circumstances, and that the outlook has changed considerably. Before 1750, or even 1756, there blew from the North-West a wind of Anglomania; but the effect of what we term the Boscawen outrage,[1] and of the Seven Years' War, was to produce a change of view. Infatuation gave way to disdain and the success of Rousseau's ideas was facilitated thereby. But this frame of mind did not last until 1789; after the treaty of Versailles a *rapprochement* began between the two countries. In agreement with Vergennes, to whose mind the treaty of 1786 was not too high a price to pay for an understanding between the Western Powers, Linguet and a few other writers aver that justice had not been done to the British Constitution, because it had not been understood. They offered it as a basis of discussion to the future lawgiver and, as I think I have shown elsewhere, many revolutionaries, deriving their inspiration from the ideas of the Whigs, accepted the

[1] *v.* Corbett, *England in the Seven Years' War* [1907], i, 52–9. On 10 June 1755 Admiral Boscawen, acting under dubious orders from the British Government, intercepted the French fleet and captured three vessels before any declaration of hostilities.

Revolution solely because they conceived it as a distant offshoot of the national conservative movement of 1688.

Another difficulty has been brought home to us recently, more particularly as a result of M. Brunot's remarkable work: that of the vocabulary. The eighteenth century was a critical period during which modern conceptions emerged little by little; but at times, men were not conscious of these novelties, and especially did not succeed in defining them clearly. A distinction is drawn between politics and administration, but this latter word is not yet prevalent, the word "police" being too often adhered to. Occasionally, to meet the requirements of study, words are borrowed from other foreign languages, but without preserving the meaning they had in their country of origin. Hence the possibility of constant error, and the need of delicate and exact investigation. For instance, the Frenchman contrasts the despotism he condemns with "enlightened" despotism. I believe neither of these words belongs to the language used in England at the time. "Ministerial" despotism is what the British condemned at the end of the eighteenth century. I had occasion, some little time ago, to devote my attention to the word "arbitrary". In the seventeenth century, of course, no depreciatory meaning attaches to the word any more than in the Middle Ages. Yet in the 'fifties of the eighteenth century, as early as Diderot, a sinister interpretation appears, and Bossuet's interpretation of the word becomes more and more confined to academical dictionaries or official documents. How can this evolution be accounted for? In order to understand it, we must go back to the English seventeenth century, when the holders of Parliamentary rights asserted the superiority of legislative Acts to royal proclamations and contemptuously described the will of the King as arbitrary, that is to say, as impulsive and wantonly despotic. In their turn, the reformers of 1756 were in need of a specific term to use in attacking the King's absolute power, the legitimate character of which they could not deny. The word arbitrary was therefore the one they chose for the purpose.

These considerations fully account not only for the gaps but for the actual errors in the sum total of our knowledge. Old positions require to be revised and an advance can only be achieved at the price of methodical studies undertaken simultaneously in our respective countries. Without entering into particulars and without attempting to forejudge the result of such investigations, the following are a few of the suggestions to which my own work has led me:

1. There can be no question but that, in the eighteenth century, the French, and more particularly the parliamentarians, paid special attention to English judicial institutions, whether administrative or legal. But what they took to be the vital element of our greatness was the idea of the law, debated in Parliament, and prevailing over the whims of the monarch. To them, strange to say, English Law stood out as a rational truth, and almost a logical consequence of the classic Cartesian spirit. Philosophers and jurists of one accord subordinate all manner of progress to the upholding of that sovereign Law, the protector of rights and safeguard of interests. But they had no particular admiration for the Parliamentary system itself, perhaps on account of the criticisms levelled against it by the Whigs, and because, to their mind, it favoured the power of the Court and cosmopolitan finance. This aversion from the system constitutes one of the fundamental elements of our revolutionary history and partly explains its developments.

2. Many of our doctrinal conceptions were borrowed from England and many adjustments were called for. The whole policy of dear wheat, for instance, and the physiocratic principles, are to be accounted for by the success of the measures adopted in England, at the end of the seventeenth century, to raise the price of corn and improve the condition of the producers. Free exports, in particular, resulted in higher prices and it was on the strength of this success that our administrators and technicians based their propaganda in favour of free trade and dear corn. Here again, the classic method of reasoning led them to consider that a measure advisable in some particular case must necessarily be successful in all. True, among Terray's friends, there were those who criticized these abstract deductions and objected that the length of coast-line and the structure of France were not similar to those of Great Britain, that our roads and waterways did not permit of a prompt disposal of our perishable goods, and that consequently absolute freedom of exchange was a delusion and a snare. The only point I wish to make in the matter is that there was a general desire to copy England.

3. On the other hand, I am still far from seeing daylight in the problem of social science, more particularly as regards insurance. Certainly it is that from 1789 to 1815 demographers evince a very lively interest in the studies carried out in England. Such men as Clavière are plainly shaped by British methods, and steeped in British statistics. And when under the Consulate and the Empire matters relating to the death-rate, the birth-rate, the census or insurance, are dealt with, attention is chiefly paid to information obtained from London. Truth to say, the question of insurance remains somewhat obscure and would deserve to be thoroughly investigated. Various documents, one of which was

published by the *Revue d'Histoire Moderne*, and certain pieces belonging to the collection that has just been sold by the Hiersemann firm of Leipzig, disclose the fact that as early as the middle of the eighteenth century, at least at such ports as Bordeaux and Bayonne, the technique of insurance had already made fairly great strides. It is desirable that the procedure should be cleared up in detail, and that the problem of reinsurance, more particularly, should be tackled.

4. It is my opinion that, were we to proceed for some distance along these lines, we should find that directly or indirectly French insurers set up close ties with London. For London, as from the middle and still more from the end of the eighteenth century, is the great market for bullion and credit, and therefore exerts a vital influence on France, an impoverished country, crushed by taxation. It is true that under King Louis XVI credit was easy, but on condition of not asking for too much, and particularly for cash. It has long been averred that even in war time French loans were partly floated in Great Britain, but my own investigations tend to show that a number of Paris shopkeepers were dependent upon the good will of your countrymen. The same applies to the bankers: in every balance-sheet I have been able to peruse the London market occupies the first rank. We are of course aware, nowadays, that the great banks at that time were owned by Protestants, and that such Geneva or Paris firms as Thelusson's had very close relations with British firms. It follows that any diplomatic tension, any threatened rupture, led to a higher rate of exchange and the denunciation of credit, resulting in the impossibility of transacting further business. What is by no means sufficiently known is the extent to which this development affected many minor enterprises, as well as the larger firms operating far

afield, and the shopkeepers as much as the bankers. There is yet another angle to the action of your country. Paris, which was then in process of development and modernization, stood in need, for its prosperity, of a large influx of foreign visitors. For the hotels, the patronage of the English appears to have been a very desirable windfall; one insolvent hotel-keeper, whose balance-sheet is preserved in the archives of the Seine Department, gives as the reason for his default the absence of that clientèle caused by the war in America.

Many another example might be adduced, and other problems set, but in doing so I should exceed both the time at my disposal and the purpose I had in view. I am not here to afford to historians such as yourselves any new lesson; I merely wished to call your attention to the many obscurities remaining to be cleared up in the study of Franco-English relations in the eighteenth century, and to the interdependence of our two countries from every point of view.

4. Anglo-French Finance in the time of Law and the South Sea Bubble

by

HENRI HAUSER

THE years that followed the Peace of Utrecht were marked in France by a shortage of credit and a widespread indulgence in speculation unprecedented in our country, a period generally described as the period of the "Système". Now at the same time, Great Britain was experiencing a similar movement. There, too, conditions are usually summed up by a reference to the "South Sea Bubbles". But though there is some suspicion of a relation between what was happening in Exchange Alley and the famous scenes of the Rue Quincampoix, and in spite of the fact that John Law hailed from Scotland, the two occurrences have usually been studied apart and without seeking to determine them, or to ascertain whether they reacted the one upon the other.

Our attention was called to the possibility of such a connection as early as 1923, by accidentally coming across a small volume, in the Widener Library of Harvard University, the full title of which runs as follows:

The Mississipi Bubble: a Memoir of John Law, by Ad. Thiers to which are added authentic accounts of the Darien Expedition, and the South Sea Scheme, translated and edited by Frank S. Fiske. New York, Townsend and Co., 1859 (Harvard Econ. 222. 15, from the Library of James Russell Lowell).

There is an error to be observed in the title: Memoir *of* John Law, the reference being to a memoir of Thiers *on* Law, published the year before, and which is thus seen to have been translated immediately in America. The term "Mississipi Bubble", used with reference to the

"Système", would naturally be understood better than elsewhere on the American soil, where matters relating to the Great Valley were current topics. The title set up a sort of parallelism between the folly of the "Mississippians" and the other "bubbles", over in London. And in order still further to stress that similarity, the publisher included under the same cover a narrative by Charles Mackay of the "South Sea Scheme". The idea was therefore rife in American circles, at the time when the gold problem arose in 1859, that the monetary and financial crisis had been as destructive in England as in France.

In the light of these ideas, and without having time to conduct any further investigations, we resumed the study of the whole subject in the usual standard works.

We found, in the first place, by a reference to Cunningham's time-honoured book, that the tide of speculation in England had set in long before 1715, and was already running high at the time of the War of Secession. Two fundamental reasons account for this rise: (a) the situation of the Treasury and the Money Market since the Whig revolution, as revealed by the founding of the Bank of England, in 1694, clearly an emergency measure; (b) the oversea expeditions to the Spanish Colonies. Some of these creations were earlier, others later than the conclusion of peace. That of the Darien Company was earlier; it may be considered as one of the prime causes of the Act of Union. It affected the shaping of Law's ideas, and, conversely, the "Système" influenced the evolution of other companies.

By this time, Davenant, Hutcheson and Defoe had denounced the rapid development of gambling on the Stock Exchange. "It appears", we are told, "to have turned the heads of everybody." Great rises and falls in prices, exaggerated profits, the success of certain com-

panies led private individuals, through the system of
Joint Stock Companies, to rush into speculation, without
themselves having to engage in business transactions,
but merely deriving a profit from the rise of the shares.
Conversely, when the value of some security declined,
all hastened to sell, thus precipitating the fall.

The new finance, and particularly the "stockbrokers",
were accused of inciting people to gamble. Their action
is described as "infamous practice". As early as 1697,
Defoe, in his *Essay on Projects*, deprecates these "fine
discoveries, new inventions, machines and what not",
and pours scorn on these "shares in a New Nothing".

It is therefore easy to understand that in 1720 Exchange Alley was a replica of the Rue Quincampoix.
London followed in the steps of Paris and *vice versa*. The
South Sea Ballads show us the Stars and Garters and the
highest ladies in the land speculating for a rise, selling
their jewels with a view to buying shares. The "quality"
speculated in the taverns, millinery establishments and
linen-drapers' shops: the famous hunchback alone was
not to be seen. Managers held open-air propaganda
meetings, floated a loan at 400 per cent. and it took
them but a few hours to collect subscriptions to the tune
of a million and a half sterling. And just as was the
case in France when the slump gave signs of setting in,
the great were the first to sell, notably the lords, who
were to accompany the King to Hanover. Pope charges
the King himself and his German mistresses with having
taken their winnings across to the Continent. Lord
Molesworth branded the "contrivers of the villainous
South Sea Scheme" as "parricides of their native
lands". In the matter of panics and ruined families,
London was a replica of Paris.

And all this had its inception in the scheme of the
Scottish clergyman who in 1695 had obtained the con-

cession of a Royal Charter "to set up a Company empowered to trade in Africa and the New World, and to plant Colonies and build forts with the consent of the inhabitants, in places not owned by other European nations". This fundamentally Scottish scheme had appealed to the nobility, the gentry, the merchants and every market-town but one; £400,000 were collected, perhaps half the hard cash in Scotland, besides the monies subscribed in England (£300,000) and on the Continent (£200,000). No doubt this operation made a deep impression on the imagination of the Scotsman John Law. The jealousy of the East India Company prompted them to oppose the establishment of this rival; they controlled the House of Commons, which decided to impeach all English agents operating for the Company. In its turn, the Dutch East India Company appealed to William III to the same end as their English rival. And it was in order to place the whole economy of the island under the control of a single Parliament that England desired and carried out the Union.

After Utrecht, moreover, England was confronted, as France herself was, with the problem of the War Debt. She received rival proposals from the Bank of England and from the Darien Company, which had now become the South Sea Company. By this time, the South Sea Company were attracted, in their turn, by Law's success, and their great scheme for the general settlement of the Debts, debated in Parliament on 22 January 1720, was inspired by the French example. The success of the South Sea Company led to the fast and furious flotation of all manner of loans. It would be wise, however, to distinguish between the real "bubbles", some of which were pricked overnight, and the many clever and productive schemes: in contrast with the quest of perpetual motion, there were schemes for fisheries, for the utilization of coal in the manufacture of iron and steel, for the draining of marsh lands, etc.

It took the disgruntled outlook of a Swift to liken Exchange Alley to an abyss in the South Sea.

What it urgently behoves us to bring out is the conflict between the "Système", as established in France by the Scotsman, and the English Scheme. Whatever may be thought of Law's financial achievement, he gave an undeniable impulse to French industry, while dire straits were the lot of English industry. With the help of Spitalfields operatives he set up a wool factory on his estate at Tancarville. He called over English glass-blowers to Harfleur, established a smelting-house on the English model at that port, another at Saint-Germain. For the Chaillot yards he engaged an English craftsman, "Jones the Gunfounder", whose brother William, who had originally remained in England, was brought over to Versailles, where he founded a watch factory, with 900 hands, for the Compagnie des Indes, and subsequently a lead foundry.

Lord Stair, a shrewd observer, is much perturbed by this exodus of workmen, reminiscent of Colbert's boldest methods. "We cannot be too prompt", he writes, "in taking the most efficient steps to prevent Mr Law from enticing our manufacturers away from England." In order to bring these craftsmen home again, he plays off Dubois, with whom he is all powerful, against Law. The Scotsman thus falls a victim to the Anglophile policy of the Régence. The Contrôleur-Général stands up in defence of his threatened offspring, and goes so far as forcibly to prevent twelve operatives, though provided with regular passports, from leaving the country.

Great, therefore, was the rejoicing in England when the depreciation of the Banque Royale's banknotes led to the homecoming of the English craftsmen. The English took advantage of this to ruin Law's industrial achievement. As early as October 1720, the Chaillot workshops were empty. There remained but two or three workmen at the Versailles watch and clock works. The new Ambassador, Sutton, was delighted at the ruin of the Charleville cloth factory. "The French", he writes, "have improved their cloth factory at Charleville to such a degree that under their guidance and instructions they might have brought it up in a very short while to the same pitch of perfection as our best English factories." It will therefore be seen that, agreeably to what M. Gaston Martin has already taught us, and the penetrating studies of M. P. Harsin reveal to us more clearly every day, the alleged "dispenser of delusions" had a liking for positive achievements. Under his management, the Contrôle-Général was not the "office of dreams" described by the legend.

The brief sketch we have drawn above would require to be completed by further details. There is no question but that the diplomatic records of France and England —not to mention other countries such as Holland— would afford us further revelations. I am confident that any investigations of this kind will confirm the view that the South Sea Company and the "bubbles", on the one hand, and the "Système", on the other, cannot be studied separately. Mutual reactions, enmities and rivalries make of these two sets of facts one and the same phenomenon, a general crisis, to wit, affecting the whole of Western Europe on the morrow of the wars of Louis XIV. Only when studied in an international light will that crisis be properly understood.[1]

---

[1] Apart from W. R. Scott's book in 1910, the following are the works we have chiefly made use of: O. Sturb, *Law's Handel und Kolonialpolitik* (Zürich and Leipzig, 1914); Michael, "Der Südseeschwindel, 1720" (*Viertelj. für Sozial und Wirtschaftgesch.* T. VI, 1908); E. Hecksher, "A note on the South Sea Finance (*Journal of Economics and Business History*, February 1931); and the studies of P. Harsin.

II

THE NINETEENTH AND TWENTIETH CENTURIES

5. English Public Opinion and the French Revolutions of the Nineteenth Century

by

ÉLIE HALÉVY

THE political history of Europe in the course of the nineteenth century may be considered as a series of insurrections against the order established by the Congress of Vienna in 1815. This order meant, in internal politics, the return, in so far as the thing was practicable, to absolutism of the type which had prevailed in Europe before 1789: in questions concerning the distribution of territories among nations it also meant the return to the *status quo ante bellum*, except for a certain number of modifications which appeared necessary, and against many of which, in fact, Western Liberalism often protested: the annexation of Genoa to Piedmont, of the Rhineland and part of Saxony to Prussia, of Belgium to Holland and of Norway to Sweden. The Mediterranean revolutions of 1820 (Spain, Portugal and Naples) were the first upheaval. They deeply impressed English opinion, and prepared the way for a new school of foreign and commercial policy under Canning and Huskisson. They did not, however, influence French politics, except that this tended at first to strengthen rather than weaken the forces of the Right. They do not, therefore, belong to my subject.

Not so the revolutions of 1830. They began in Paris, where in three days the legitimate monarchy of Charles X was overturned, and Louis-Philippe, Duke of Orleans, was made "King of the French" in his place. Then, just as in 1820 the insurrection in Spain had spread to

Portugal and Italy, the insurrection in Paris spread to Switzerland, Hesse, Hamburg, Saxony, Brunswick, Belgium; and from Belgium it spread to England, where it brought about the passing of the Reform Bill.

I know that this is not the way in which the story of the passing of the Reform Bill is usually told in England. It is presented as the natural outcome of an indigenous agitation in favour of a more or less radical reform of Parliament, which began as early as the eighteenth century, was nipped in the bud by the wars with revolutionary France which followed, sprang into existence once more as soon as peace was restored, and lastly, after years of active propaganda, produced the Reform Bill. Now, it is true that the "radical" agitation was intense in the years which followed the return of peace, more particularly during the years 1817 and 1819; and that round about 1820 everybody considered that the existing electoral régime was doomed. But it was then that Lord Liverpool rallied to a more liberal conception of Toryism, with the result that when, in 1828, an economic crisis broke out which was more serious than the crises of 1816 and 1819, there was no radical agitation, and no demand for electoral reform: the country was obviously satisfied with Canning's and Huskisson's moderately liberal Toryism. Again, it is quite true that, after the passing of the Catholic Emancipation Bill in 1829, the question of Parliamentary Reform was revived. But it was a complicated and confused agitation, not to be compared with the far more serious agitation which had convulsed the country ten years earlier. It was started by Tories (the Marquis of Blandford and Attwood of Birmingham), who complained that Catholic Emancipation had been forced by a minority upon an unwilling majority, and hoped that a more democratically elected Parliament might be inspired by more genuine Tory feelings. The result was that the Liberal press expressly disowned all sympathy with the movement. When the general election began, at the end of July 1830, as a result of the death of King George IV, the only question which raised any enthusiasm was the abolition of slavery: the country as a whole was apathetic; never before had a smaller number of seats been contested.

Then came the insurrection in Paris, and the change in England was dramatically sudden. The insurrection was too popular for anyone, even Wellington, to dream of supporting an expedition by the Allies to restore the fallen monarchy; there was hardly one insignificant Tory paper to speak of him, when he came to seek a refuge in England, with the slightest touch of sympathy. But, in spite of the fact that Wellington himself had at bottom little sympathy with Charles X's and Polignac's dreams of territorial aggrandisement towards the Rhine and the Mediterranean, he was considered by everybody and could not but consider himself as *solidaire* with Charles X; and the fall of Wellington was the natural outcome of the fall of the last of the Kings of France. After which came the Reform Bill: it was not the bill drawn up by Lord Durham upon a purely French model, it was, in its final form, something different, in one respect more timid (there was no ballot), but in all respects far more bold. Does anybody quite realize to-day that Louis-Philippe's France, with thirty million inhabitants, only had a quarter of a million electors, while the United Kingdom of Lord Grey and Lord Melbourne, with twenty-five million inhabitants only, had about eight hundred thousand electors? And the fact remains that there would probably have been no Reform Bill in the years immediately following the death of George IV, that there would at all events have been no measure to be compared for its boldness with Lord Grey's bill, if it had not been for the French Revolution of July. Such was, at that time, the international solidarity of parties. We have here a most interesting example—and one which is quite exceptional in the history of England, of an important historical event being the direct repercussion of an event in continental, and more particularly French, history.

The next European upheaval happened in 1848. It did not really originate in France, as is too often believed by French historians. It began, in 1847, with the civil war in Switzerland: it spread to Italy, at the beginning of 1848, with the Sicilian insurrection, and the concessions hurriedly made to liberal claims by all the sovereigns in the Peninsula. The experts expected the revolutionary movement to spread all through Germany. In France, they expected nothing more than a riot, which would be successfully crushed by the modern Ulysses. Things went the other way. In a few hours' time, Louis-Philippe was swept off from his throne as Charles X had been eighteen years earlier: and manhood suffrage was established in France. Then the movement spread to Germany, with successful insurrections in Berlin and Vienna, the King of Prussia accepting a constitution, the Emperor of Austria in flight, Metternich vanishing for ever from the scene, and a Parliament in Frankfurt looking for some way of unifying Germany upon a democratic and liberal basis. What then of England?

The position in England may, in many respects, be compared with what it had been in 1826, a little more than twenty years before. England, from 1837 to 1842, had gone through domestic troubles analogous to those of the years 1817 to 1819: a suffering working class was appealed to by agitators, now called Chartists, who once more preached the old doctrine of Universal Suffrage. Then, from 1842 to 1846 the movement had been not crushed but appeased by that great "Conservative" statesman, Sir Robert Peel, who had brought forward a programme of economic as opposed to political reform. Close upon the Bank Act of 1844 and that bold move, the repeal of the Corn Law in 1846, had come, in 1847, a most severe commercial crisis; just as Huskisson's and Robinson's reforms had been followed by the crisis of 1825: and just as the crisis of 1825 had left the political atmosphere undisturbed, and the radical agitators unpopular and neglected, so also the crisis of 1847 did not in any way diminish the popularity of Sir Robert Peel (who happened in fact to be out of power at the time, through the accidents of party policy) and did not provoke even the beginning of a revival of Chartism.

Suppose there had been no Revolution of 1848, would perhaps events in England have taken such a turn as to make a further, and more radical, Reform Bill necessary? The thing does not strike me as probable. Not only because nothing of the kind would have happened in 1832, if it had not been for the Revolution of 1830; but also because the Reform of 1832—thanks to the Revolution of July—had been so bold as to go beyond the real desires of the population. Is it true, on the other hand, that the Revolution of February exerted something of the same influence which the Revolution of July had exerted, and accelerated the march of Reform in England? We may admit that when Lord John Russell—"Finality Jack"—acting in 1852 as Prime Minister, made electoral reform the main point in his programme, events in France influenced his design; but we must not forget that the attempt failed badly, and that nothing more was heard of it for many years; and we must not forget either that democratic France had just surrendered herself into the hands of a military despot, and that the events in France and elsewhere, which from the beginning of 1848 onwards disturbed the fear of Europe, were of a kind to teach England a lesson which she was not slow to learn.

The Revolution of 1848 had, as its first result, a revival of Chartism. The crisis of 1847 had left it dormant; in March and April 1848 it was alive once more. But, although in the industrial North the movement was fairly serious, and led to trouble and bloodshed, in London it ended, as everybody knows, in the most pitiful and ridiculous of fiascos. In the Sister Island, it gave rise to graver trouble: why not (thought the agitators on the other side of the Irish Channel) a free Ireland as well as a free Hungary, a free Italy, a free Germany? But the only result, at the time, in England, was to harden the common feeling against all concessions to radicalism. Not that the reading of the daily newspapers is perhaps the best way to understand what the feelings of the English people were: the events were so crowded, the judgments passed on them necessarily so confused. The *Morning Herald*, a Tory paper, having been the only paper in London to predict a successful French revolution, chose to write hopefully of the probable outcome of the republican experiment in France. The *Morning Chronicle*, an ex-radical paper which had gone over to Peelism, from June onwards threw in its lot with Louis-Napoleon. But there is no doubt about the general feeling. Everybody, irrespective of party, was proud to belong to a nation which had, for more than a century, escaped the opposite excesses of revolution and reaction, and in particular the peril of reaction through revolution; proud to belong to a nation strong and stable enough to receive all those who fled from

Paris, Louis-Philippe, most despised of refugees, and Guizot, and Louis Blanc some months after, and Ledru-Rollin one year later, all in their turn the victims of the passing moods of the crowd. It would not be true to say that England, at this time, was proud of her own "revolution" of 1832, whose boldness she did not understand, the more so because the French had just been making a bolder experiment. The Reform of 1832 now appeared as having been nothing more than a cautious adjustment to altered circumstances of the political régime established in 1688. In moderate liberalism, combined with a policy of radical free trade, England felt that she had found the peace and safety after which France, and indeed the whole of Europe, was unsuccessfully groping. The current feeling, engendered in England by the Revolution of February and the convulsions which followed, was of conscious and proud opposition to the French methods of government.

The next upheaval in Europe is more difficult to define and to date. The revision of the "treaties of 1815" happened less as a result of popular insurrections than of wars undertaken by adventurous statesmen—Napoleon III, Cavour and Bismarck—who had taken a leaf out of the book written by Canning and Lord Palmerston, and understood that the popular and patriotic outcry for liberty might be used to forward policies of national aggrandisement and prestige. Four great wars, the Crimean War, the Italian War, the Sadowa and the Sedan War, changed the face of Europe, and inaugurated that era of democratic militarism, which, upon a new basis gave Europe forty years' respite from war. If, however, one were asked to point out one particular year as being the critical year in the history of this European revolution, 1870 should undoubtedly be chosen as being the year which saw the achievement of the unity of Germany, upon its foundation of manhood suffrage, the unity of Italy, with the fall of the temporal power of the Pope, and the establishment of a democratic republic in France.

France, in the years which followed her bad defeat, made the interesting attempt to build up a constitution upon the English model: an experiment the more interesting because the new constitution had to be based upon manhood suffrage, with no possibility of an appeal to the hereditary principle. The thing was not done on purpose; it happened in an assembly which had not been elected to make a Constitution, "under the dictatorship, as a contemporary says, of circumstances". The result was not even a Constitution in the proper sense of the word, preceded, as had been the rule since 1787, by a declaration of abstract principles, but a bundle of five or six separate laws, bearing on different points which might have been the chapters of an authentic Constitution. You expect England to take some interest in so English, so "un-French" an experiment. In fact it took none at all. Very few were those who sympathized with the work accomplished by the Assemblée Nationale.

Freeman, writing in 1874 at a time when the Assemblée had not yet even sat down to build a Constitution, far from deploring the delays, expressed the hope that the French were at last learning a lesson from England, and perhaps beginning to understand that you can do without a written Constitution. But can such an eccentric estimate of the situation be taken seriously? In fact, it was belied by the event. There had been, on the other hand, even before 1870, a small body of Englishmen who were proud to call themselves republicans. But their number was insignificant, their attitude was that of a political dandy rather than of a a doctrinaire, eager to be taken seriously; and after the downfall of the Empire, when the first act of a government which was, provisionally at least, non-monarchical, was the sanguinary repression of a Parisian insurrection, their sympathies were with the Communards, not with the men who, after having slaughtered them, happened to wish to make France a republic. Such men as Frederic Harrison, head of the British positivist school, believing as they did in the future of the French Republic, did not for a moment stoop to admit that the institutions created in 1875 by the Assemblée Nationale would be lasting institutions. They were the fraudulent work of a reactionary assembly, and would infallibly be overhauled as soon as Parliament became republican in spirit, as well as in name. As for public opinion, taken as a whole, it had no faith in the prospects of French Republicanism.

Nobody understood that the so-called "Constitution of 1875" was to be the most successful, the most lasting of the many French experiments in constitution-making. The general impression was that France was sooner or later to fall a prey to some sort of military dictatorship. Not that anybody cared very much. I was startled to find, in studying this period, how much sympathy was felt for Napoleon III in England after his military disasters and political downfall. Was this the effect of an incipient fear of Prussia? Or was it a chivalrous feeling of what is due to a defeated captain? Or a strong disapproval of the way in which the French people after remaining faithful to Napoleon so long as he was successful, had suddenly found it convenient to drop him on the day of defeat? Or was it again the remembrance of all that he had done, often in opposition to public feeling, in order to maintain as close an entente as possible between the two nations? Whatever the explanation, the fact is there. The time had passed when international parties fraternized irrespective of frontiers; the time had passed when liberal England, proud of her liberal institutions, would have rejoiced to see them spreading over the world, and wondered only whether other nations were worthy of adopting them and making them living realities. Quite indifferent as to the more or less democratic, more or less military, forms of government under which the new Europe was choosing to live, England would have been ready to put up with French Caesarism, if she could have been sure that it did not spell war. Her only anxiety was peace.

In short, English feeling as to the three successive revolutions in France was, in 1830, sympathy; in 1848, conscious hostility; in 1870, total indifference. The evolution of public opinion in this respect may be said to have obeyed a law of increasing insularity.

6. Lord Palmerston at Work, 1830–41

by

C. K. WEBSTER

WE have begun to inquire more closely into the methods by which public affairs were carried on in the nineteenth century. Foreign policy, for example, though directed by the Secretary of State, was the product of a number of different processes carried out by an official machine. We need to know the exact share played in them by the Crown and the Cabinet, the control exercised over them by Parliament and the Press, the relations of the Secretary of State to his permanent staff both at home and abroad.

These matters are not always easy to ascertain. They do not appear to a great extent in the ordinary correspondence of the office. We learn them from marginalia on despatches, e.g. the comments of the Crown, from drafts, from private correspondence of Cabinet ministers, members of Parliament, ambassadors in London, who often comment upon and explain the processes by which foreign policy was determined, though sometimes inaccurately and with much prejudice against particular persons. For later years the minutes of the office are preserved and we can see from the publication of Dr Gooch and Professor Temperley how revealing these are. For the first half of the nineteenth century, however, the machinery of the office was not so systematized. Some description of these processes has been attempted

[1] This was originally published in *Politica*, August 1934. It was part of an address at a meeting of French and British historians at the Sorbonne on 26 March 1934, on "The British Diplomatic System in the First Half of the Nineteenth Century". I have added further illustrations and references.

by Professor Temperley and myself for the years 1812–27.[1] Less is known of the period immediately succeeding. An interesting collection of papers in the Record Office, however, throws considerable light on Palmerston's methods of work. In the *List of Foreign Office Records* they are described as "Minutes, Memoranda, etc., Lord Palmerston".[2] Written on quarto or octavo double sheets, they were obviously often attached to the despatches and documents on which they comment. They are now detached, but notes by the Under-Secretary often enable us to determine the papers to which they refer. Sometimes they were notes passing from the Foreign Minister to his Under-Secretaries, either from one room of the office to another, or from his town house or country residence to Downing Street. The majority of them are Palmerston's drafts of answers to despatches, nearly always complete in detail except for formal beginning and end, sometimes, in the more routine answers, merely an indication of a well-established formula which could be at once used by the clerks. Amongst them, however, are a number of minutes by Palmerston himself or his Under-Secretaries—John Backhouse, Sir George Shee, and the Hon. W. T. H. Fox-Strangways, which throw much light on the working of the machine.

They demonstrate, if it were necessary, the complete knowledge and control of the Foreign Minister over all the details of his work. As Palmerston explained to the young Queen, when she inquired with some *naïveté* as to

[1] In his *Foreign Policy of George Canning*, 1822–27, and my *Foreign Policy of Castlereagh*, 1812–15, and *Foreign Policy of Castlereagh*, 1815–22. A recent paper by E. Jones Parry, "Under-Secretaries of State for Foreign Affairs, 1782–1855" (*English Historical Review*, April 1934), contains much new information. There is also a short account of the Palmerstonian period in *The Foreign Office*, by Sir John Tilley and S. Gaselee.

[2] F.O. 96, *Miscellanea*, Nos. 17–20 contain the papers of this period. Where no other reference is given below, this series is indicated.

what was "bureaucratic influence": "In England the Ministers who are at the head of the several departments of the State, are liable any day and every day to defend themselves in Parliament; in order to do this, they must be minutely acquainted with all the details of the business of their offices, and the only way of being constantly armed with such information is to conduct and direct those details themselves". He contrasted this state of affairs with some exaggeration with that existing elsewhere: "On the Continent, where Ministers of State are not liable so to be called to account for their conduct, the Ministers are tempted to leave the details of their business much more to their Under-Secretaries and to their chief clerks. Thus it happen[s] that all the routine of business is generally managed by these subordinate agents; and to such an extent is this carried, that Viscount Palmerston believes that the Ministers for Foreign Affairs in France, Austria, Prussia and Russia, seldom take the trouble of writing their own despatches, except, perhaps, upon some very particular and important occasion".[1] Palmerston here was hardly fair to the industrious Metternich, but certainly these documents reveal a minute and unceasing examination of all the routine of the correspondence by the Secretary of State such as is not apparent in other countries. But light is also thrown upon more important matters. We can trace, for example, exactly what was done with the incoming despatches and in particular how they were circulated to the King and Cabinet. Backhouse answered to an inquiry of Palmerston's, apparently provoked by some complaint, as follows: "According to the established rule

[1] Palmerston to Queen Victoria, 25 February 1838. *Letters of Queen Victoria*, ed. A. C. Benson and Viscount Esher, I, 136. The drafts of the Austrian instructions preserved in the Staatsarchiv at Vienna show how much Metternich wrote himself. But more was written for him than for Palmerston.

of the office the Despatches are sent to the King as soon as they are sent back to the office by Lord Palmerston and are sent to Lord Melbourne as soon as they are returned by the King".

To which Palmerston indignantly replied: "This is an idle innovation since last year. The practice during the Four Years previous to November last [when Melbourne's first Ministry was replaced by Peel's for a short space] was that all despatches of interest and importance were copied as soon as returned by me, and the originals were sent to the King and the copies to the Prime Minister. This practice, the discontinuance of which I have never authorised, should be forthwith revived.

"It is preposterous that the First Lord of the Treasury should be kept in ignorance of despatches till they have gone down to Windsor and come back again. If Lord Melbourne happens to be a few miles out of Town himself this may keep him three or four days in arrear."[1]

King and Prime Minister saw all official despatches of importance, some not sent to other ministers, especially those of a more delicate nature. Thus a minute on Lamb's "secret" despatch reads: "This is to go only to the King and Lord Grey. I take it to be a 'Metternich'"',[2] a comment which reveals also Palmerston's opinion of the influence of the Austrian Chancellor on his ambassador, who by no means accepted all the ideas of his chief with enthusiasm.

How necessary it was to have the despatches copied immediately on their arrival was seen in another incident. For when Palmerston asked for some papers he found they were at Howick, and Backhouse hastily

[1] Minutes Palmerston, 11 and 12 October 1835. Minute [Backhouse], undated.
[2] Minute Palmerston, 26 January 1833. On another occasion: "Send Lamb to-day copies of anything not sent to him and which there can be no harm in Metternich seeing". Minute Palmerston, 26 February 1832.

excused himself by alleging that there was not time to copy them as they had only been received from Palmerston "a short time before the post hour on the evening on which they were to be sent to Lord Grey".

On which Palmerston replied: "...they ought not to have been sent off so far as Howick without retaining copies; no original despatch ought in any case to be so dealt with; besides all risks on the road, I am thus deprived of the despatch for nearly a week. I desire that this may never happen again".[1]

This was all the more necessary because all the Cabinet had the right to see all the despatches, though, as we have seen, some were withheld from them. Certain ministers received special treatment, obtaining the despatches immediately after the Prime Minister, and ultimately all were placed in the Cabinet Room at the Foreign Office, of which all the Cabinet members had the key. The process is shown in the following minute by E. Hammond: "...The despatches which arrive from abroad go 1st to the King, then to Lord Melbourne, then to Lord Holland, and then upon the Cabinet Table. As long as Lord Lansdowne was in town the despatches were sent to him before being placed on the Cabinet Table, and they will now be sent to Sir John Hobhouse in consequence of orders I received yesterday to do so".[2]

When ministers were out of town, however, they could not go to the Cabinet room, and other means were invented by Palmerston to keep them informed. He introduced a system of abstracts of despatches, which were supposed to be sent out every day, presumably by post, to every member of the Cabinet not in

[1] Minute Backhouse, 1 October 1833. Minute Palmerston, 2 October 1832.
[2] Minute E. Hammond, 1 October 1835.

Town. The office groaned under this duty and it is clear that Palmerston's colleagues frequently complained that they were not getting as many as they considered they ought. Backhouse was profuse in apologies: "I am sorry to say that the abstracts for Members of the Cabinet, although commenced agreeably to your Lordship's order have been very irregularly continued—principally from sheer want of time and hands to make them as well as the copies required for the King *on the day* of the arrival of despatches—when they happen to be detained by your Lordship till a late hour of the day—or not to arrive (as is often the case) till a late hour.

"The only way of securing such abstracts on all occasions would be to have them made before the despatches are forwarded to Your Lordship. For myself I will gladly undertake to make them (so far as relates to despatches arriving early in the morning) if Your Lordship acquiesces in the delay which may be necessary for that purpose, before the despatches are sent to you. But with respect to the evening work of the clerks when despatches of consequence arrive, I do assure Your Lordship that with our diminished numbers (from absences) and with the great increase of copying required of late, it is often quite impossible to accomplish the necessary work within the proper time...."

That an Under-Secretary of State should offer to do such work shows not only his zeal but throws a vivid light on his conception of his duties. Apparently also he was the only member of the office whose constant practice it was to be there in the morning. We know from other sources that it was only with difficulty that the Clerks were induced to appear by noon. Palmerston, however, insisted on the work being done: "This certainly shews great increase of copying labour—but if the abstract cannot go on the very day to which belong [*sic*] they should be sent the next morning".[1]

Complaints, however, continued, and Palmerston again called for a return, which resulted in a new set of minutes. Backhouse had various excuses—"the belief that the Ministers were in Town", and the fact that "Mr Staveley and Mr Hammond, on whom the business of making abstracts devolves, when I am prevented doing it myself, have had their hands so full that there was no leisure for doing that which was not considered indispensably necessary". But Palmerston would not be put off. "How long is it", he asked, "since an abstract was sent to Lord Carlisle or Lord Holland?" "The transmission of these abstracts is not registered," replied Backhouse, "but none appear to have been since the reassembling of the Ministers." "I wish in future", minuted the Secretary of State, "that the sending of these abstracts should be punctually attended to and that they should be invariably sent to every Cabinet Minister out of Town. Lord Carlisle did not come to Town, and the assembling of his Colleagues was no reason for cutting him off from all knowledge of what was passing abroad." Backhouse passed this on to Sir George Shee with the suggestion that some machinery was necessary "in order to ascertain what Ministers *are* out of Town". Sir George Shee had also sent an explanation to Palmerston of his share of the transaction: "Nothing of political importance has arrived in my branch during the past week. What did arrive as the Ministers had returned to Town and assembled in Cabinet I sent to them in circulation boxes".[2] Thus

[1] Minute Backhouse, 28 March 1833. Minute Palmerston, in reply.
[2] Minute Palmerston, 6 December 1833. Minute Backhouse, 7 December 1833. Minute Palmerston, 7 December 1833. Minute Backhouse, in reply. Minute Backhouse (for Shee), 8 December 1833. Minutes Sir George Shee, 7 December 1833.

apparently some despatches were circulated to all
ministers before being sent to the Cabinet room, if the
Ministers were engaged in Cabinet meetings, and this is
confirmed by other Minutes of Palmerston: "These
despatches and drafts should be circulated and read by
the present Cabinet beginning with Lord Melbourne",
though this may refer to past history; and on another
occasion: "Let care be taken that this despatch is seen
by each member of the Cabinet".[1] The circulation of
abstracts however, continued for a considerable period.
They were even sent to Lord Lansdowne by the
ambassador's bag when he was in Paris.[2] Palmerston
took up the question again when he returned to office,
for he found his colleagues (most of whom were not too
glad to see him back at his old post) full of complaints
on the subject. This time Backhouse's answer was that
nothing worthy of abstract had arrived. The three clerks
specially responsible, Hammond, Mellish, and Ward,
furnished some not altogether convincing details on this
point. Hammond added the explanation quoted above
of how the despatches were handled. Palmerston's
decision was: "A bulletin should be sent every day even
if it is to say there is no news"; so another avenue of
escape was cut off.[3]

This practice was later discontinued,[4] possibly when
the printing machine was more used. The printer was
used during this period for long memoranda and despatches, but not as a matter of routine, so far as I can
discover, until near the end of the 'thirties, when "the

[1] Minutes Palmerston, 4 May 1835; 3 November 1835. The latter refers
to an important draft *to* Lord Durham.
[2] Minute Palmerston, 27 October 1834.
[3] Series of minutes, 29 September–2 October 1835.
[4] Lord Broughton (*Recollections of a Long Life*, ed. Lady Ilchester,
v, 15) noted on it: "a very convenient holiday practice which has since
been discontinued". The Irish despatches were treated in the same
way.

most important despatches" from London seem to have been circulated in this manner some time after they had been sent off.[1]

There is also some information on the correspondence outwards. The important drafts were of course submitted to the King. One minute throws some light on Palmerston's methods. "I do not feel quite sure", wrote Backhouse, "whether this draft to Lord Granville falls within the class of those which Your Lordship wishes to be submitted to the King before they are sent abroad." "Yes", replied Palmerston, "but I always wish to see my own drafts again before they go to the King, as the probability is that a Mem. hastily written will require a good deal of cutting and hewing."[2] The King's alterations were not often of great moment though occasionally we find on the drafts in the Record Office annotations on phrases. On one occasion these were not noted, being made on an inside page.[3]

There is one record of the King's curious suspicions which were directed to both France and Russia, evidence of his unbalanced mentality. Palmerston inquired: "The King wishes me to instruct Bankhead [Chargé at Washington] to endeavour to ascertain the nature of some secret articles which he conceives to be annually

[1] Palmerston ordered 100 copies of a Memorandum on Spain to be printed for the Cabinet before the meeting of Parliament. "The Printer thinks", reported Backhouse, "that by working day and night and all Sunday he may be able to supply the copies on Monday afternoon." He hinted that the order of a 100 implied a wider circulation to the Memorandum than was prudent unless it was "pruned" by Palmerston himself, as, though not secret, it contained "an exposition of the crooked policy of the French Cabinet". Palmerston therefore reduced the order to twenty-five copies but "keep the Press standing". Minute Backhouse, 28 January 1837. Pencil note by Palmerston.

[2] Minute Backhouse, 9 December 1836. Minute Palmerston, in reply.

[3] Minute Backhouse, 21 November 1836. The King had written his usual "Appd." at the top of the despatch and so deceived the Under-Secretary. Subsequently when he made an alteration he always wrote "Appd. subject to the amendments below".

renewed between France and the United States. Do you know anything of the existence of such articles; and could such a communication be made to Bankhead with certainty of its not being read by the U.S. Government?" To which Backhouse replied: "1. We have no intelligence whatever of any such secret article as H.M. supposes.

"2. There would be no difficulty in getting an instruction safely to Bankhead's hands by means of the monthly Halifax and Boston Packet and by the employment of a special messenger by the Consul at Boston for the conveyance of the despatch from that city to Washington.

"I have shewn the note to Mr Vaughan [British Minister to the U.S.A.]. It accounts to him (he says) for a summons which he received last night from Sir H. Taylor to attend the King to-morrow morning—of which summons he came (dutifully) to apprize Your Lordship.

"Mr Vaughan never heard of any secret article and he thinks that a secret treaty renewable every year and therefore necessarily communicated every year to the Senate for its sanction could not possibly remain a secret at Washington".[1] Palmerston, though he appears to have attached some importance to this strange enquiry, had already begun to treat the Crown in the manner which was later to make him so famous. For an early minute runs: "...let me have this for signature by one. The Draft may go to the King without a date to it and he will not know it is gone."[2]

Sometimes the King's alterations were made through the Prime Minister, showing that they had discussed the draft together.[3] I have only found one reference to the

[1] Minute Palmerston, 30 May 1832. Minute Backhouse 31 May 1832.
[2] Minute Palmerston, 1 September 1832.
[3] Minute Palmerston, 28 February 1834. On this occasion the King insisted on substituting the word "*communication* with Russia upon a common object" for "*co-operation* with Russia for a common object".

King's conversations with foreign representatives and this apparently one of those done at Palmerston's instigation, and not on his own initiative which sometimes led to surprising results.[1]

The young Queen had not in this period begun her criticism of the drafts. Prince Albert became her secretary after her marriage, but he took some little time to get going. Though she read the despatches diligently she was treated by the Foreign Secretary and the Office with some gallantry, but not very seriously. "The less you send the Queen this next week beyond what is necessary for her to see the better", minuted Palmerston—"as her time will be much occupied by Ascot."[2] Another minute from Windsor asks for "the most interesting despatches of last month" to be sent to him, a request which caused some annoyance, as they were all over the office in the clerk's rooms and led to the minute: "The *interesting* and *romantic* despatches keep till tomorrow when we may perhaps have a Messenger to send down".[3]

Both Grey and Melbourne had of course to be treated more seriously. There are two or three instances of Grey altering drafts. He certainly kept a check on them while in London. But he found it difficult to keep up with the correspondence and we find him asking the office to make him *précis* so that he could get up a situation quickly. Moreover, he would go down to Howick and it was difficult to control Palmerston from a spot so far away. There is no

---

[1] Minute Palmerston, 30 March 1834. Tricoupis, the Greek Minister, submitted for Palmerston's approval the despatch in which he described the King's remarks as highly hostile to Russian influence in Greece.

[2] Minute Palmerston, 10 June, 1838.

[3] Minute Palmerston, 26 September 1837. Minute G. Lennox, 27 September 1837. Minute Fox-Strangways, in reply.

allusion to alterations by Melbourne, perhaps a significant piece of evidence.[1]

The Under-Secretaries, as the previous minutes have
revealed, were no more than clerks and did not inter-
fere in matters of policy.[2] There was no distinction in
duties and status between Backhouse, the permanent
Under-Secretary, and Sir George Shee and Fox-Strangways, the two "Governmental" Under-Secretaries, who
were appointed by Palmerston himself, the forerunners
of the later Parliamentary Under-Secretaries. The two
Under-Secretaries still divided the countries of the world
between them, for the old division of North and South
still persisted. But they also divided between them the
duty of supervision of the whole office. Palmerston's
demands were so insistent that one of them had apparently always to be present when the Secretary of
State was himself in London. Thus we find several notes
from Backhouse as to his absence on Sundays, week-
ends, or longer leave, always explaining, however, that
he would remain until his colleague had arrived.[3] When

[1] Grey to Palmerston, Monday [31 January, 1832]; 6 March 1832.
There is, of course, much evidence in foreign archives on the relations of
Palmerston with Grey and Melbourne which I cannot go into here. Grey
was extremely vigilant about the instructions to Durham in 1832, but
perhaps that was an exceptional case. Lord John Russell stated in 1840:
"In the days of Lord Grey every important note was revised by him and
generally submitted to the Cabinet. As Paymaster of the Forces I had then
more information and more power of advising than I have now".
(Spencer Walpole, *Life of Lord John Russell*, 1, 363.) But this was written in
a moment of great irritation.

[2] Cf. also a note of Shee to Backhouse in 1832: "Lord Palmerston, you
know, never consults an Under-Secretary. He merely sends out questions
to be answered or papers to be copied when he is here in the evenings, and
our only business is to obtain from the clerks the information that is
wanted". (Tilley and Gaselee, *The Foreign Office*, p. 3.)

[3] Thus Minute Backhouse, 1 April 1831, asking permission to leave
on Sunday evening because of his father's illness: "I say Sunday evening
because Sir Geo. Shee says that he proposes to go into Hertfordshire
tomorrow, and it is indispensable that the office should not be left without
the presence of one of us".

Cabinets were summoned an Under-Secretary and other clerks had to be at the office on Sundays as well.[1] The two Under-Secretaries were, indeed, so indispensable and hard worked at times, that they alternately remained almost permanently on duty or recuperated in the country.

"Backhouse and Strangways", wrote Palmerston to Granville, "are very much like the two figures in the Weather House and rusticate and labour alternately, so that if the office were left vacant for a short time, it would only be as if one of the two were in the country recruiting from his fatigues."[2] This was at a moment of great tension but there is some evidence that Backhouse, the permanent Under-Secretary, had already begun to establish the superiority of that office over that of the "Governmental" Under-Secretary. By far the greater part of the minutes are from his hand and though this may be accidental, since the other Under-Secretary probably took his own special papers away with him, yet it seems likely that it was on Backhouse that Palmerston mainly relied in normal times for the running of the office machine. Of the Under-Secretary's zeal and industry there can be no doubt and even when away ill he entreated to be kept informed of the work of the office.[3]

[1] Minute Backhouse, Sunday, 14 August 1831: "May I ask if your Lordship will want any clerks on my side of the office this afternoon? I have one here now who is assisting in copying the Brussels despatches for the Cabinet. I shall remain here whether specially wanted or not until I am relieved by Sir Geo. Shee at 4 o'clock". Palmerston replied: "I do not think I shall want anybody but when a Cabinet is summoned there is no telling". This brings out very clearly the position of the Under-Secretaries each specially responsible for their own half of the globe, but relieving each other of the duty of supervision of the whole.

[2] Palmerston to Granville, 22 November 1839. *Granville Papers*, Box 14.

[3] Backhouse to Fox-Strangways. Ryde, 26 August 1835: ' . . . I cannot say I feel much benefit as yet. . . . P.S. May I beg you to have the goodness to cause to be sent to me occasionally . . . a selection of any despatches of

Over the clerks themselves Palmerston exercised an
unremitting control and discipline, which explains why
Greville thought they might illuminate the Foreign
Office when he lost his seat for South Hampshire in
1835. He does not seem to have realized the pain which
his vigorous minutes sometimes caused nor to have
always taken the circumstances fully into account. On
one censure for an apparent error Backhouse protested:
"I cannot omit this opportunity of stating to Your
Lordship how grievously Mr Cuningham has been disturbed at the apprehension of the omission (of which he
was not conscious) and at Your Lordship's Minute upon
it, which he understood as implying a charge of wilful
neglect of his duty...". To which Palmerston cheerfully
replied: "I am very glad the mistake did not occur
because it might have had a very inconvenient effect
upon our relations with Spain, and, as it did not occur,
of course, my remarks fall to the ground and have no
application".[1]

But it must be remembered that Palmerston was
always over-worked. Correspondence and interviews
and Cabinet and House of Commons kept him con-
tinually on the wheel. He answered his despatches with
great regularity and promptitude though occasionally
he had to plead pressure of work as a reason for delay.[2]
He would sometimes finish an important expedition by
staying at home and thus avoiding interruption. This

special interest which have been received since my departure and
especially of the instructions addressed to our missions abroad...".

There is a minute of Palmerston's, apparently during this same illness,
2 September [1835]: "Send Backhouse's letter to him. The large packet
I suppose contains the secret bulletins. These should be addressed in the
future to you while Backhouse is absent". These were probably reports
from Paris.

[1] Minute Backhouse, 13 October 1832. Minute Palmerston, 13
October 1832.

[2] There were, however, complaints at times, e.g. from Sir G. Villiers,
cf. Sir H. Maxwell, *Life of Clarendon*, I, 101.

explains to some degree his terribly bad habits of un-
punctuality and not keeping engagements. Thus when
Backhouse, in a little note, pointed out that the King's
Advocate, who had called by appointment, had been
waiting an hour and a half, Palmerston replied: "I am
writing a draft which I have long been prevented from
doing from day to day. If once I come to the office I am
lost for the day. Do talk to Jenner and get his opinion.
You know the case, it is simple and you can explain it
to him...".[1]

Yet, as is well known, he always had time and energy
for other things than business. One minute here indeed
asks that the next Messenger to Calais shall enquire for
"8 pieces of stuff for gowns, belonging to Lady Cowper
and to bring them to England as they cannot go into
France".[2]

When so hard pressed it was not easy to bear with the
slackness of subordinates. "It is utterly impossible for a
Secretary of State", he wrote of another error, "to bear
such things in his mind, and it is the duty of those in his
office, in whose department the business may be, to look
after these matters of punctuality and routine."[3] But
he knew that the office was not really slack, though it
might have that reputation. "Some answer or acknowledgement ought always to be sent to every application
when it is received", he once admonished them, "in
order to shew that due attention is paid in the office to
communications made to it. When Parties who apply
are allowed to remain for many weeks without any reply

[1] Minute Backhouse, 25 June 1832, ½ past 4 p.m. Minute Palmerston,
in reply. On another minute asking for an appointment for General
Alava, Palmerston replied: "5 is my hour always; after the Cabinet"
30 January 1839.
[2] Minute Palmerston, 15 December 1833. He added that he would pay
the charges.
[3] Minute Palmerston, 18 May 1837.

they naturally go about saying how idle and inattentive the Foreign Office is—not knowing the cause which has delayed the final answer, and the office thus gets a character the very reverse of what it deserves."[1] More than most ministers he felt a reflection on the office as a personal one: "It ought to be a standing and invariable rule of the office to give some answer or acknowledgement to every letter received, and it is especially necessary to do so with regard to a letter referred to the Queen's Advocate who sometimes keeps references for two years. It is very disagreeable for me to be blamed individually in the House of Commons for omissions which arise from inattention on the part of the clerks in the office to the elementary routine of business".[2]

How far the clerks responded to these strictures is a matter of doubt. Judgment would no doubt depend upon the standard applied. But Palmerston was able, on quitting office, to take leave of his subordinates in language which is far from a mere routine expression of approval of their efforts. He even averred in 1851 that their "ability, intelligence, industry, and zeal have made the Foreign Office a model Department".[3]

To the Diplomatic service his attention was just as assiduous. His remarks on their handwriting, spelling, and composition have become proverbial. There are many other instances of these criticisms in these minutes, some referring to caligraphy and ink, but others even more wounding. Prolixity and the use of Gallicisms were his particular aversions.

Two of his ministers in South America were to be told "private" his wish "that after they have written their despatches and before they have them copied out for

[1] Minute Palmerston, 2 November 1836.
[2] Minute Palmerston, 23 July 1840.
[3] Sir E. Hertslet, *Recollections of the Old Foreign Office*, p. 64.

signature they would run them over and strike out all words which may not be necessary for fully conveying their meaning".[1] When one of them continued to offend, Palmerston wrote: "If Mr Hamilton would let his substantives and adjectives go single instead of always sending them forth by Twos and Threes at a time, his despatches would be clearer and easier to read".[2]

This was the more necessary because the correspondence of the office was increasing at an enormous rate. It more than doubled during this period.[3] This was partly due to Palmerston's determination to keep his representatives well informed. He never forgot one of the cardinal points of diplomacy, viz.: that good information can only be obtained by well-informed agents. Consequently he circulated far more despatches than his predecessors.[4] He paid constant attention to this point himself and was well aware of its importance. Thus during the Wellington ministry the messenger to St Petersburg was abolished owing to its great expense, and, when Palmerston inquired as to the effect of this, Fox-Strangways pointed out that "so long as the steam packets run in the Baltic Mr Bligh can hardly fail of finding some English traveller going to Hamburg who would be most happy to take charge of his despatches in consequence of the facilities which a courier's Passport secures to him for his journey". Palmerston replied: "But if a secure mode of sending despatches had been established Mr Bligh might have been furnished with more copies of communications to and from other

[1] Minute Palmerston, 3 July 1835.
[2] Minute Palmerston, 4 August 1835.
[3] Despatches sent out 1829, 3,470; 1840, 8,979. About double the number were received. In each case about one-third were Consular and Slave Trade. *Accounts and Papers*, 1857–8 (417), XI, 31.
[4] Backhouse drew attention to this point (28 March 1833) and gave figures ("I speak of my own branch only") 1829, 200; 1831, 707; 1832, 1566.

Courts".[1] As a rule secret and private despatches were
not sent abroad but exceptions were made, and Palmerston ordered the substance of them to be circulated as
reliable secret information received at the Foreign
Office. Granville was specially allowed to receive
nearly everything, including many secret and private
letters.[2]

If he was vigilant in pressing the secrets of his own
correspondence, it was partly no doubt because he had
no illusions on the practice of the day of opening all
letters. It was indeed his habit to take advantage of this
fact when he wished to convey to a foreign Government
some particularly nasty observations which he could not
very well send direct. Mr Addington, however, was
sufficiently naïve to believe that such practices were not
countenanced by English-speaking Governments. "He
declared", reported Backhouse, "his *perfect conviction*
that the Correspondence might be so transmitted
[through the American Post Office] without danger:
the Americans, said he, are no more up to such Austrian
tricks than we are." He seemed to trust the Spaniards
in the same way. "You had better open his eyes",
wrote Palmerston, "on this practice of opening letters
in Foreign Towns and tell him that when he means to
read the Spanish Government a lecture this is a good
way of doing so."[3] Even William IV used the expedient
to enlighten a brother monarch: "The King wishes this
letter to the Duke of Cambridge to be sent so as to be

[1] Minute Fox-Strangways, undated. Minute Palmerston, 8 September
1835. The Petersburg Messenger cost, in 1834, £632. 16s.
[2] Minutes Palmerston, 11 October 1833; 29 July 1834; 13 November
1835; 31 October 1836. A minute of 3 November 1837, illustrates his
constant attention to this point: "In the present insecure state of the
roads in the North of Spain, it may be prudent not to send Mr Villiers
copies of any very confidential despatches from Ministers of other Courts,
especially from Lord Granville".
[3] Minute Backhouse, 23 May 1831. Minute Palmerston, 23 May 1831.

sure of being intercepted and read by the Prussian Post Office: what would be the best channel through which to send it?"[1] In England also, of course, letters were opened in the same way and there is more than one reference to intercepts in these minutes.

He took pains also over the personnel of the Diplomatic service. Patronage was still the only means of selection. The number of unpaid attachés had grown enormously —to such embarrassing dimensions, indeed, that no one knew how many there were. They were apt to come home on indefinite leave from places they did not like. Palmerston tried, not altogether with success, to establish the rule that they should obtain permission first. Over the paid attachés he took considerable pains. Thus before allowing a transfer to Vienna he made quite certain that the applicant could not only read German but also German script. Both he and Backhouse were also interested to see that the attachés had proper training in the Foreign Office before going to posts abroad.[2] There is of course nothing in these minutes about the higher appointments, for such discussions would not have been suitable for office eyes.

In the Palmerstonian period the increased supply of Blue Books on Foreign Affairs, which Canning had begun, was greatly augmented. There is ample evidence in these minutes of how carefully Palmerston himself supervised the documents which were to be laid before the Houses. He himself often indicated the passages of the despatches which were to be omitted. He was also constantly directing that information should be supplied to the Press. *The Globe* and *Morning Chronicle* were at this period the two papers most favoured, but he also paid

---

[1] Minute Palmerston, 13 November 1832.
[2] Minutes Backhouse, 27 April, 12 October 1833; 8 January 1838. Minutes Palmerston, 16 April 1833; 2 May 1837; 2 November 1838.

particular attention to *The Times*. There are two examples of direct action both in his own handwriting. The first merely lays down "the tone for *The Times* to take about the acknowledgement of Maria", and is careful to avoid the appearance of Government inspiration by concluding "but let them especially avoid speaking otherwise than in their own persons or as having any other lights than their own reflections".[1] The second is headed "For Globe Friday" and is a short leader obviously meant for insertion as it stood, written to warn the public against subscribing to a loan to Uruguay, whose Government had refused to sign a treaty of friendship and commerce with Britain.[2] The assertion that Palmerston wrote leaders himself, which has been doubted, is here proved to be true.

Of Palmerston's gusto and energy in attention to the smallest details of administration these papers give ample evidence. Whether he is urging a drastic reduction in Passport fees so that British subjects may use them in preference to those issued free by France; or choosing a present for the Turkish Ambassador, a pair of double barrelled guns and a pair of pistols "to be looked for at John Moore at the bottom of St James Street"; or suggesting that someone should be sent to a sale to see if some advertised correspondence of Lord Healey did not belong to the Foreign Office; or ordering that "to prevent the filching of leather covers for the Boxes they should be stamped with the words 'Foreign Office'", and protesting, when his orders had been carried out, "I do not admire the taste of the gigantic Shop Inscription Letters"; or enquiring, "Why are these Mail Bags not put up so as to be protected from water? I wish it to be ascertained whether Packet Captains are ordered

[1] Minute Palmerston, undated [1833].
[2] Paper in Palmerston's handwriting, Saturday, 24 October [1835].

always to stow the Mail Bags below. I have reason to believe that these Bags are allowed to remain on deck"; the Secretary of State always knew his own mind quite certainly and demanded prompt action from his subordinates.[1] "One instance is as good as a hundred", he informed Fox Strangways, who excused himself for delaying a protest, on the ground that he was "only waiting for a few more cases".[2]

Such exuberance and energy obviously needed a worthier setting than the block of private houses in Downing Street that composed the old Foreign Office. Palmerston was already planning a new building. There was no need for an official residence for the Secretary of State, he informed the Treasury. Canning was indeed the only occupant of the post who had lived in the office. But it must contain two large rooms for his dinner parties "upon Birthdays and occasionally upon the arrival of Foreign Princes in this country". "Upon such occasions", he added, "the number of guests is nearer 50 than 40, and it must be obvious to Treasury that there are very few private houses in London which could afford the means of entertaining such parties."[3] The new Foreign Office, when it came, bore the impress of his masterful personality, but not all Palmerston's energy could bring it into existence in his lifetime, and he was never able to dispense hospitality in the rooms which he had planned.

[1] Minutes Palmerston, 3 May 1831; 7 February, 19 June, 9 September 1833; undated [1833]; 24 April 1836.
[2] Minute Fox Strangways, 22 September 1835. Minute Palmerston, 23 September 1835.
[3] Draft prepared to Treasury, 25 May 1836.

7. The Annexation of Savoy and the Crisis in Anglo-French Relations, January–April 1860

by
G. PAGÉS

THERE can be no question here of a comprehensive survey of the diplomatic crisis brought about in 1860 by the annexation of Savoy to the French Empire. The scope of the present paper is far more restricted. The "Cerçay Papers",[1] taken by the Germans in 1870, and returned to France under the Versailles treaty, include a fairly large number of personal letters written by Persigny to the Foreign Minister, Thouvenel, during his second embassy in England, and showing us the various stages of the crisis as seen from London. While bringing to light very few new facts, they deserve, it would appear, to be known, because they contribute to a better understanding of some of the reasons of the crisis, and particularly of the Parliamentary and psychological reasons.

Our sole aim is to make known to historians these unpublished letters of Persigny's, though of course they only shed light upon certain stages of the crisis. The allusions to be found in them would hardly be intelligible were we not to have present to our memory the whole succession of events between January and April 1860. It has therefore been considered necessary, in the first place, to give a clear and concise account of what we know of the crisis from the writings of English, French, Italian and Swiss historians. It will then be possible to revert in somewhat greater detail to the points as to which Persigny's letters contribute a few new and definite facts.

[1] v. infra, p. 88. A short description of these papers is in *Les Origines diplomatiques de la Guerre de 1870–1*. Tome XIII. Paris [1921] App. III.

In the conversations at Plombières, Napoleon III had been led by Cavour to expect that if he assisted Piedmont against the Austrians in Italy, he would be able to annex Savoy and the County of Nice to the French Empire. The secret treaty of January 1859 recorded this promise, but it remained subject to one condition: Italy to be free as far as the Adriatic seaboard. Napoleon was aware, therefore, that he was giving up the projected annexation when, on 11 July, he unexpectedly concluded the Preambles of Villafranca, leaving Venetia to Austria. But nobody, at the time, looked upon the Italian problem as settled by this transaction: neither Cavour, who resigned from the Ministry, the better to provide for the future; nor Napoleon III, though he first attempted to stabilize the incomplete results of the war, by organizing an Italian Confederation; nor Franz Joseph, who was not resigned to defeat. It was inevitable, therefore, that Europe, and more particularly England, should be perturbed.

The concern of the English Ministry is evinced, as early as November 1859, in a well-known letter from Lord Palmerston to Lord John Russell; it troubles people's minds long before the beginning of the year 1860. Until January, however, the matter that gives concern to governments and diplomatists alike is not the question of Savoy—which had not yet been raised—but recent developments in Italy, and the solution of the Italian question as a whole. It was with a view to the settlement of the Italian question that the abortive scheme for a Congress was mooted and given up; that the French Government sought for information at Vienna and Saint Petersburg, as well as in London; that they eventually suggested to the English Government an understanding, the conditions of which are set forth in the famous Palmerston Memorandum of

5 January. It does not fall within the scope of this paper to examine how that projected understanding, to which Lord Palmerston was certainly favourable, came to be abandoned; or how Lord John's "four points" were substituted for it on 15 January; we will merely remind our readers that the sole aim of those proposals was likewise to prepare the settlement of the Italian issue, and that there is no reference in them to the question of Savoy.

The period of expectancy lasted for some weeks. True, indeed, as early as 4 January the appointment of a new Foreign Minister in France had foreshadowed a new trend of the Emperor's policy: Napoleon III accepted Walewski's resignation and chose Thouvenel to succeed him. But Thouvenel, at the time, was Ambassador at Constantinople and, pending his return, Baroche was appointed *ad interim*, and for some time the Anglo-French conversations were proceeded with on the basis of Lord John's "four points"; they could lead to nothing. Moreover, the sole concern of the British Cabinet, which was none too secure and was subjected to many assaults in the Commons, was to postpone all difficulties; nor was it willing to impede the conclusion of the commercial treaty then being negotiated in Paris by Cobden. It was only on 20 January that events began to move more rapidly. On the 20th, Cavour resumed the leadership of the Piedmontese Cabinet. On the 23rd, the Anglo-French Commercial treaty was concluded. On the 24th, Thouvenel's return put an end to Baroche's temporary appointment. Lastly, on 25 and 27 January, two articles in the *Patrie* suddenly called the attention of the public to the question of Savoy. This time the crisis was under way.

There are several stages to be observed in it. The first covers the whole of February. As soon as Thouvenel arrived in Paris, Napoleon III consulted with him, and the result of their conversations is recorded by the minister in a Memorandum, which he must have submitted to the Emperor by 26 January at the latest. In this, Thouvenel points out two possible solutions to the Italian problem: either the creation of an independent kingdom in Central Italy, or the adjunction of the Duchies to the Kingdom of Sardinia. He adds, however, that this latter, which he obviously deems the more likely arrangement, would not be devoid of advantages for France. "It must necessarily involve the adjunction of Savoy and the County of Nice to France", he writes, "by virtue of the same principle as that which will have made the fortune of Piedmont. The soundest of reasons would in that case make this rounding off of our territory imperative for the security of our frontiers. It would be a *sine qua non*, and what must be done is to prepare the public and the several Cabinets for this development." This new policy finds its earliest expression—though a secret one, like the Memorandum—in an autograph letter from Napoleon III to Victor Emmanuel, drafted on 27 January, and handed in by Talleyrand to the King of Sardinia on 2 February. In this letter, Napoleon suggests, like Lord John, "four steps", but which are not completely identical with the "four points" of the English statesman. While admitting the principle of non-intervention; while advising Victor Emmanuel "boldly and frankly to give up all idea of further encroachments on neighbouring States"; while adhering to Lord John's suggestions in permitting "a general vote of the Central Italian provinces", he advises the King of Sardinia (his fourth suggestion) to "grant to Savoy and the County of Nice the same freedom as in Tuscany" and to "conform to the wishes of the freely consulted populations". It will be seen that there is perfect agreement between the sovereign and his minister.

During the whole of February, however, the policy of Napoleon III develops on two different planes: on the one, the Emperor does not entirely diverge from his original conception and seeks a solution by way of compromise, at least in Tuscany and the Romagna; on the other, he accustoms himself to the idea of giving way at every point, provided he gains Savoy and Nice. But the feeling of uncertainty remains. In Italy, the situation only becomes somewhat clearer after Cavour has flatly rejected a sort of ultimatum, contained in a despatch from Thouvenel, dated 24 February. In England the policy of the Palmerston Ministry is no clearer; it is dominated by current Parliamentary difficulties, by the desire to obtain from the Commons a prompt ratification of the commercial treaty (it was duly ratified on 10 February), lastly by anxiety not to provide the Opposition with the opportunity for too virulent attacks. In consequence, Lord John Russell strives to prevent the Savoy issue from being debated in Parliament, vouching for Napoleon's good intentions. The last assurances thus given by the Secretary of State to the Houses of Parliament date back to 28 February, two days before the Emperor's speech on 1 March, which tore down the veil.

We may sum up very briefly the second and third stages of the crisis, because Persigny's despatches will oblige us to revert to them frequently. The second stage —a very short one—covers 12 and 13 March. It begins on 12 March, by a speech of the Emperor's at the opening of the Parliamentary session. In that speech Napoleon III announces and states the reasons for his decision to claim from the King of Sardinia the cession of Savoy and the County of Nice. "Confronted with a transformation of Northern Italy giving a powerful State possession of all the passes through the Alps, it was my duty, for the security of our frontiers, to claim the Western slopes of those mountains." Thereupon, he engages in a negotiation at Turin for the purpose of obtaining the King of Sardinia's consent to a plebiscite in Savoy and at Nice, in case Central Italy should be adjoined to Piedmont, but without waiting for the actual union to be consummated. The *pourparlers* soon resulted in a Franco-Sardinian treaty, bearing the date of 12 March. It was a secret treaty, publication of which was deferred until 24 March. As from the 13th, however, a circular addressed by Thouvenel to all diplomatic agencies imparted an official character to the designs of Napoleon III. The third stage, in fine, comprises the most critical period of the crisis and its termination. It is marked, in so far as the relations between France and England are concerned, by a very sharp incident that occurred, on 27 March, between the Emperor and the English Ambassador, Lord Cowley, during a concert at the Tuileries; then, in the House of Commons, by violent outbreaks against the Napoleonic policy, and a speech by Lord John Russell on 25 March; lastly, on 27 March, by a confidential talk between Lord Palmerston and Count Flahault, who happened to be in London at the time. The crisis lasted, with the same degree of sharpness, until the end of April. But from this time onwards Napoleon unswervingly pursued his policy, which culminated in the plebiscite of 18 April at Nice, and that of 22–23 April in Savoy.

We will now glance at the letters of Persigny, as well as at a few other private letters, also addressed to Thouvenel, and included with them in the "Cerçay Papers".[1]

Some of these letters (not from the pen of Persigny)

[1] v. *supra*, p. 83.

disclose to us the way in which the Emperor's agents abroad were in formed of Walewski's retirement, and how the transition from the old policy to the new was effected. A letter of Talleyrand's is very enlightening in this respect. The following is what Talleyrand writes to Thouvenel from Turin on 23 January:

"For you to realize the uncertainties, the thick fog surrounding me. I must tell you that at 6 p.m. on 4 January, M. Walewski sent word to me that I was to leave, and in the morning of 5 January, at the station book-stall, I bought the *Moniteur* calling you to Paris. By good fortune I found myself, here, in the midst of a Ministerial crisis, and my silence, in presence of people doomed to be swept away, may possibly have redounded somewhat to my credit. But the case is no longer the same. We now have to deal with a real Ministry, and a real Minister; and if I can keep to an attitude of reserve just for a few days more without being written down a fool, I shall have reached, I fancy, the extreme limit of their indulgence. There is urgent need of you calling me to Paris to give me my instructions...."

It thus becomes easy to understand the paralysis with which the Imperial policy would appear to have been struck during Baroche's temporary appointment, and many further proofs of which are to be found, for instance, in the private correspondence of Montebello, Ambassador at Saint Petersburg. Obviously, in the development of the new policy, the period from the 4th to the 24th of January counts for nothing. In London, Persigny is left to his own devices, and to one of his moves, as it happens, he refers in one of his letters, that of 26 January. In this we see that he had something to do with the original idea of Lord John Russell's four points. He had just been informed that Austria had rejected the English proposals, while secretly binding herself not to intervene. This was a matter of surprise to him:

"It must be confessed", he writes, "that Austria's method of reasoning is a strange one. My chief aim, in suggesting the system under which France and Austria would jointly be bound not to intervene, apart from the European Concert, was to save the military honour of Austria.... To those who told me that she would refuse to agree to the proposals, I replied that in doing so she would expose herself to the alternative, eventually, of suffering a humiliation or committing a folly; but she goes one better—it is now—at once—that she waives the folly and appears to accept the humiliation."

The first question that occurs with reference to the Savoy issue is the following: how were the English Government, how was the Queen made cognizant of the plans of Napoleon III? We know already that just before the middle of January 1860, Prince de Joinville warned Prince Albert, who could hardly fail to warn the Queen. He drafted, for his own use, a Memorandum which has been published. But we find traces of a far earlier warning. It comes from Persigny, who had a talk with Lord John Russell, in the early days of July 1859. On 5 July, Lord John Russell imparted to the British Ambassador in Paris, Lord Cowley, the words of Persigny, and this letter of 5 July was inserted in a Blue Book. Now Persigny's private correspondence confirms and defines the facts. In a letter to Thouvenel, dated 3 February 1860, to which we shall have occasion to revert, Persigny refers to the fact that he had broached the question of Savoy in London, in his own name, "long ago". Subsequently, in a further letter, dated 28 March, to which we shall also revert, he unreservedly confirms the statements of the Blue Book. Speaking of the assurances given by Walewski to Lord Cowley at the time of the Preambles of Villafranca, to which the English had just referred, he expresses his surprise at finding that Walewski had behaved so incautiously, and he contrasts his own attitude with that of the late Foreign Minister.

"For my part", he writes, "I raised the question in London on my own responsibility, I introduced it in my own name and supported it in every possible way, and as you will see by Lord John's despatch in the Blue Book, quoted just before Lord Cowley's..., I put the matter on its proper footing."

The attention of the English ministers was therefore awakened as early as July 1859. A rather important difference is to be noted, moreover, between the language held by Persigny, and that held by the Prince de Joinville. The latter spoke confidentially in January, of the desire of Napoleon III to reach "the natural frontiers" of France, at least along the Alps. This, no doubt, was the expression that alarmed Prince Albert and the Queen. They both refer to it, the former in his Memorandum, the latter in a letter she wrote to Lord John Russell. The allusion to the "natural" frontier along the Alps, inevitably suggested another "natural" frontier, that along the Rhine. But this was not at all the way Persigny had expressed himself. He merely referred to the danger with which France would be threatened by the formation of a powerful Italian state, unified and in control of all the western slopes of the mountains. That is what he describes as putting the matter on its proper footing; and the words he had used were identically the same as those employed later on by Napoleon III in his speech to the Chambers on 12 March 1860. There was, therefore, in the language of Prince de Joinville (and without his sincerity being in any way open to question) a tendencious interpretation of the Napoleonic policy which gave rise to anxiety throughout Europe. This it was that rendered necessary, and at the same time ineffective, the denial issued later on by Thouvenel in his Circular of 13 March.

The private correspondence of Persigny reveals to us the position taken up by the Ambassador in London at the outset of the crisis, and brings home more clearly the nefarious consequences of the articles in the *Patric*. In January, Persigny is rejoiced at the accession of Thouvenel to the Ministry and at the instructions he is given: "Here at last", he writes, "we have affairs conducted as they should be". He is equally pleased at the reception accorded to Thouvenel's explanations by Lord John Russell. "Credit should be given, moreover, to Lord John", he writes on 28 January, "for always being very honest and straightforward in his dealings with us." But then come the articles in the *Patrie*. They have a deplorable effect in London. But they are also the occasion of a letter from Persigny, on 3 February, which is of importance because it clearly expounds the policy commended by Persigny and which, it would appear, would also have been that of Thouvenel, had not the same influences that suddenly caused the semi-official Press to intervene, imposed upon him a more impatient and less skilful policy, the policy, to wit, that let loose the crisis. The following are the chief passages of that letter of 5 February, which needs no comment.

"Ever since your accession to the Ministry, I had experienced a feeling of satisfaction, which you cannot but have noticed. I found the new Ministry setting forth the Emperor's policy so plainly and so skilfully; the order and succession of affairs being pointed out so methodically, that at no period of my Embassy here had

I experienced so deep a feeling of security. The question of Savoy had been particularly well expounded in accordance with your instructions. That issue, which I had myself raised long before, and by no means fruitlessly, as you may have been informed by the Emperor, you had advised me to discuss in my private talks, but in my personal name only, and completely shielding my own Government, until such time as they should deem it advisable themselves to disclose their intentions. Nothing could have been wiser and more practical, or more likely to further our aims. And now, almost at the very moment when you were commending to me so wise and skilful a course, the semi-official press must needs abruptly and unconsiderately reveal the aims of our policy, and in lieu of a dignified and distinguished attitude, which made everything not only possible, but easy, we ourselves wantonly create a situation full of dangers and difficulties, reverting to that fatal system of sudden and unforeseen publications, of premature and ill-timed revelations, the sole purpose of which would seem to consist in preparing our opponents to resist our aims...."

Persigny wonders for whose benefit such publications can be intended:

"For the benefit of Lord Palmerston's Cabinet? But could the Cabinet possibly be more favourable to us, more willing to facilitate our arrangements? And in any case, are we likely to carry it along with us by compromising it *vis-à-vis* its Opposition? Surely it would have been possible at least to await the discussion of the Commercial treaty, and was it for us to supply weapons to the opponents of a Cabinet with which we are preparing such great things?...

"I therefore advise you to request the Emperor to issue an immediate disavowal of the semi-official papers. But as that disavowal cannot possibly be a positive one, the following, in my opinion, is the spirit in which it would be appropriate to draft it. You might declare in the *Moniteur* that the Government thoroughly disapprove of the discussion started by certain newspapers with reference to Savoy; that true to his moderate and disinterested policy, the Emperor has no designs upon Savoy; that if developments in Italy were to lead to the triumph of a new nationality in the Peninsula, it might well happen that Savoy, a small country of French origin, after serving as the fruitful and glorious germ of a conglomeration of half French, half Italian states on either side of the Alps, should no longer be willing to belong to a purely Italian state, with which it would no longer have any real interests in common; and that in this case, but in this case only, it would only be fair for that small country to have a voice in its destiny, as the various fractions of Italy would have; but that any other way of dealing with the question—if so be that there is to-day a question of Savoy—would be quite contrary to the intentions and views of the French Government."

In a postscript, Persigny continued as follows: "I have just seen Lord John Russell for a brief moment. I found him, as I fully expected, very much concerned at the situation resulting for the Ministry here from the articles in the *Patrie*. He told me that he quite understood that such a question might arise eventually, in the case of a Kingdom of Italy being constituted, but that to raise it now would be tantamount to upsetting the Ministry and repudiating beforehand all the hopes England at present entertains of a friendly understanding between the two countries".

And his conversation with Lord John Russell further moved him to add this marginal note in his own handwriting: "Thus propounded on the basis of nationality, the question would raise a storm in Europe".

Among the reasons that account for the attitude then taken up by the English Government, due importance should be ascribed to Parliamentary considerations. In January 1860, the Ministry, whose existence was as yet anything but secure, apprehended all that was of a nature to supply arguments to the Opposition. Until 10 February, they feared for the commercial treaty. They also feared for their own fate. Of this, as we have just seen, Persigny was well aware: "The matter was one of great concern to me", he writes in a letter on 11 February, because it was liable to upset the Ministry; and for two days they themselves thought they were doomed". That same letter of 11 February, and others with it, afford us some light as to the conflicting influences by which Lord Palmerston was surrounded:

"My letter to-day (11 February) is with reference to Savoy. Strictly between ourselves, M. d'Azeglio's behaviour is very objectionable. He makes the greatest show of friendly feelings towards me. But Lady Shaftesbury (a daughter of Lord Palmerston), I have it on good authority, uses such violent language, and Lord Shaftesbury has assumed so hostile an attitude *that no one questions the exalted influence acting in the matter.*"

And on the 20th, he adds a few further particulars:

"By reason of his very close relations with Lady Shaftesbury—Lord Palmerston's daughter—d'Azeglio, to my mind, is the unquestionable, obvious cause of all the passions that bestir themselves round Lord Palmerston. You can hardly imagine how high those passions run. There is no mansion in the whole of London where greater unfairness and violence are indulged in against the Emperor, than at Lady Palmerston's. Granted that Lord Palmerston has nothing to do with all this: In his presence, people are generally careful not to show themselves in their true colours; yet these passion-laden surroundings are not of the best for that statesman's mental balance."

Of course, the anxiety and irritation were still greater in London after the Emperor's speech on 1 March. A debate was started in the Commons on 5 March, and of this Persigny informs Thouvenel the same day:

"The debate proceeds with the utmost passion. You can have no conception of the violence and fury of private conversations on the subject. Naturally, discussion in Parliament is on the same level....Jealousy, irritation and violence break out on all sides. It is necessary for us to be very careful to avoid all irritating discussions....I would mention that I have had some very hopeful conversations with M. Gladstone, Lord Palmerston, Lord John and Mr Bright."

The attitude of the English Government, however, is not to be explained merely by Parliamentary considerations. Account must also be taken of certain moral reasons, which do not escape Persigny's notice. On two occasions, during the crisis, the Imperial Government behaved in such a way as to lay themselves open to a charge of breach of faith. The first of these was when they reverted to their plan for the annexation of Savoy after disclaiming the intention for some time. On the eve of the Preliminaries of Villafranca, on 8 July 1859, Walewski, when questioned by Lord Cowley, had positively stated that Napoleon III harboured no thought of claiming Savoy. This was true, at the time, since Napoleon himself, by suspending operations, had forgone the advantages conferred upon him by the secret treaty of January 1859. The statement, however, was nevertheless very unwise, for circumstances were liable to alter, and the English looked upon it as a binding promise. Lord John recorded it in a speech in the House of Commons on 12 July. Accordingly public opinion in England was much perturbed by the publication, in the Blue Book, of the despatch in which Lord Cowley reported the assurances given him by Walewski:

"In all the official or semi-official correspondence disclosed to the public", writes Persigny on 28 March, "there is but one point that struck it, but it is a very serious one. I refer to despatch No. 4 in the Blue Book, by which Lord Cowley informs Lord John, on 10 July, that the Emperor has given up all idea of joining Savoy to France."

A further political change of front was also looked upon by the English, and not without good reason, as a breach of faith. In January, Napoleon III let it be understood that if he annexed Savoy, he might retrocede the Chablais and Faucigny districts to Switzerland. Thouvenel, in his turn, made a similar declaration to Lord Cowley, though in cautious terms: in his opinion, the cession of Savoy "should not necessarily entail the abolition of the clauses relating to the neutralization of the Chablais and Faucigny districts"; and he added that "with a view to imparting further strength to them, it would appear desirable to us that those districts should be made over definitely to Switzerland". And what was still more serious is that he made the same communication to Kern, the Swiss minister in Paris, on 6 February, and shortly afterwards to the Federal Council, by the intermediary of the French chargé d'affaires. But Napoleon III soon found that though fairly substantial, this concession failed to pacify either Switzerland or England, and that it might even imperil the success of the plebiscite. So he gave up the idea. Unfortunately this change of front had a lamentable effect in England. We are apprised by Persigny's letters of what was thought of it in London. It was considered that a promise had been given, and that it ought to be kept.

Truth to tell, subsequent confidences on the part of Persigny and Thouvenel present the facts in a somewhat different light. "Just before 20 March", it was alleged, Persigny, in compliance with an order received from Paris, again offered to London the retrocession of the Chablais and Faucigny districts, on condition the English Government should agree to the annexation of the remainder of Savoy to France, and it was only upon the English Government's refusal that the Emperor decided to send Benedetti to Turin, to obtain acceptance there of the conversion of the secret, into an open, treaty. These statements on the part of Persigny and Thouvenel are commented upon at some length in a footnote to M. Luc Monnier's book, *L'Annexion de la Savoie à la France et la politique suisse.* Unfortunately no confirmation of them is to be found in Persigny's correspondence, whether official or private. On the contrary, among the letters from Persigny to Thouvenel dating from before 20 March, that of the 15th is evidence that at this latter date Persigny had received no new instructions, since he himself recommended a different procedure, which, moreover, was open to more than one objection. The proper course, in his opinion, was first to obtain from Piedmont the cession of the whole of Savoy, and then to submit to the vote of the inhabitants of the Chablais and Faucigny districts the question of their retrocession to Switzerland. In a letter on the 17th, Persigny repeats his suggestion and seems to take Thouvenel's assent for granted:

"As regards the present issue", he writes, "I am glad to see that you are willing to favour an arrangement with Switzerland as regards the Chablais and Faucigny districts, after their actual adjunction, either through a decision by Europe or through a vote of the populations concerned. There must be no beating about the bush in the necessary and unavoidable step of having Savoy made over to us by Piedmont;...but for the rest, we have pledged our word and must keep it faithfully."

In any case, Persigny makes no mention of any offer such as he is alleged to have made to Lord John Russell, and which is supposed not to have been in keeping with what he wrote to Thouvenel. And on 20 March, the situation certainly does not seem to have changed.

"The reasons I imparted to Lord John", he writes, "seemed to impress him; the state of Europe is also of a nature to give him pause....Believe me, try and make a concession....It appears to me that it might be possible to cede the Chablais district, which, bordering as it does upon the Lake of Geneva, would appear to Switzerland in the light of a security."

Finally, a letter of 23 March would seem to clench the matter. The following are the chief passages:

"My reason for not attempting to see any of the English Ministers to-day is that I have nothing further to tell them and that I have got to the end of my instructions."

Persigny regrets not having been informed of the secret arrangement concluded at Turin; he is of opinion that if he had known of it, he could have prevented Palmerston from following the blind alley to which he had committed himself.

"Things being as they are", he proceeds, "I can see but one course to follow, and that is to make a sacrifice in England's favour. As a matter of fact, and however honourable may be the reasons that compel the Emperor to retract his promise to England in the matter of the Chablais and Faucigny districts, a promise given and taken back is a very serious incident in such a negocia-tion as the present one....It therefore appears to me that if—having regard to the moral conditions of

England, to the situation of a friendly Cabinet, which we have already upset once, to the good-will of Europe, and to our relations with Switzerland—we were to effect a compromise, and make over the Chablais district to Switzerland, we should be crowning a big triumph by an act of wisdom and moderation, which would be infinitely more valuable for the Emperor than this unimportant district."

And he adds in a postscript:

"I should be much obliged if you would impart these remarks to the Emperor. The matter is a grave one. I ask and pray the Emperor to think it over seriously. I am convinced it presents an enormous interest for him. I earnestly hope you will share my opinion on the matter, and commend it to His Majesty."

The next day, however—24 March—at Turin, the secret Franco-Sardinian agreement was made public.

From that time onwards the correspondence of Persigny discloses, as between the ambassador and the minister a disagreement that causes them to drift gradually farther and farther apart. It was at this juncture, as we have seen, that Persigny became aware of the assurances given to Lord Cowley by Walewski before the Preambles of Villafranca, and that in the House of Commons Lord John Russell delivered a very violent speech against the Emperor's policy. Persigny grew anxious: "What appears to me to be fraught with gravity", he writes on 28 March, "is the opinion of the country itself, which is far more incensed than I should have thought, not indeed by the annexation of Savoy—about which it concerns itself very little—but because it considers that throughout this transaction, we have acted disloyally and trifled with England". Persigny is himself indignant at the bad faith or consummate clumsiness of Walewski; and he further writes in the self-same letter of 28 March, to which we have referred several times:

"What! He waived Savoy, unconditionally, while well aware of the condition. Meanwhile, I, who knew nothing, who had not the slightest inkling of the secret treaty, or of the Emperor's designs on Savoy, broached the question in London, of my own accord.... See that a denial is issued.... Bring out the fact that as far back as 5 July—nay long before that—I had raised the question here. And that is the vital point. If on 8 July, Walewski had said what I was saying here—that the Emperor laid no claim to Savoy, in spite of the cession of Lombardy to Piedmont; but that if Sardinia became a big state we should have to claim Savoy—if Walewski had told the truth, like I did, the vexation of the English Ministers would have counted for nothing, and the English public at large, having no cause to charge us with deceit and trickery, would laugh at their Ministers, and would be on our side. Please submit these remarks to the Emperor."

We are not told whether or not Thouvenel submitted Persigny's remarks to Napoleon III. Suffice it to say that no account was taken of them. And that was the end of the trustful co-operation between ambassador and minister. Interesting evidence of this is afforded us in the shape of a private letter, dated 7 April, in which Persigny sets forth his policy for the last time, and which bears in the margin, in Thouvenel's own handwriting, the remarks it suggested to him. It is worth quoting here:

"Your private letter, permit me to tell you, grieved me considerably. If we persist in keeping everything, and reaching the Lake, we can but create a lamentable situation [*marginal note by Thouvenel*: 'Is it possible for us to make over Thonon after the address of the

municipal authorities']. This is the first occasion since
1815 on which France has openly defied England. That
is a tremendous fact, a fact that creates a sensation
throughout Europe and restores to us for the first time,
in the eyes of the world,. our full liberty of action, of
which we had been deprived since 1815. From this
point of view, the annexation of Savoy is therefore a
signal victory for France, and we should be happy and
proud of it; but the more valuable the victory, the less
we should jeopardise it by any excess.

"Now I must tell you frankly that once we had
pledged ourselves to cede the Faucigny and Chablais
districts, it is putting ourselves into an invidious position to go back upon our promise [*marginal note*: 'No
promise was ever given, but the mere expression of a
favourable intent, which was conditional upon, or
implied in, the wishes of the populations']. No doubt
we have a reason: the interests of the populations; but
for that reason to be valid, it would be necessary that
those interests should be obvious to the whole world,
and this is not the case. Nay further: even granting the
existence of those interests, Europe would be entitled
to make them give way to a higher interest [*marginal
note*: 'That higher interest not being the neutrality of
Switzerland, which no one challenges, what can it be,
save to inflict an annoyance upon France!'].

"Turning to France, I am not of opinion, either,
that a concession on the part of the Emperor would
astonish the public [*marginal note*: 'I am convinced of the
contrary']. I consider myself as good a Frenchman as
anybody else, but it is just because I am a good Frenchman,. and devoted heart and soul to the Emperor, that
I would have him give proof of wisdom and moderation.
Moreover I do not see that France can have any interest
in being on the Lake, if we are to have neither fortifica-

tions nor buildings there. It is my opinion that a cession of the shores of the Lake for the purpose of freeing the remainder of the neutral territory from binding obligations would likewise be to our advantage.

"I think you are quite right not to wish to commit yourself until after the vote of the Turin Parliament and the vote of the populations have decided the annexation; but, afterwards, a compromise appears to me to be absolutely necessary [*marginal note*: 'We should in that case have wantonly deceived the populations in promising there would be no dismemberment']. England is armed and she is stricken to the heart. Now if, not content with triumphing over her, we are further bent upon humiliating her by refusing any compromise, and this for a matter of such small importance, we are in danger of committing to chance the great victory we have won over her [*marginal note*: 'We cannot be held responsible for the effects of the attitude it has pleased the English Government to adopt towards us, in a matter which affected none of their immediate interests'].

"Last night I saw M. de la Rive, who is a friend of General Dufour and is sent here by Switzerland. I found him very moderate. He gave me to understand that General Dufour has several plans which, while taking as little as possible away from us, would leave us the possibility of forming two Departments, with Mont Blanc as part and parcel of one of them. I fancy we should eventually be called upon to make over but a narrow strip along the Lake [*marginal note*: 'The Lake is certainly a better frontier than this imaginary line']. Sensible people in Geneva are themselves undesirous of receiving a great deal, M. de la Rive observed to me, for fear of the Roman Catholic Party. I of course told M. de la Rive that I knew nothing of my Government's intentions.

"To-day I had a short note from Lord John, telling me, as I informed you by telegram, that understanding you are averse from holding any Conferences before both the Sardinian Population and the populations have registered their votes, he suggested that before any ulterior Conference we should come to an understanding as to the guarantees to be extended to Switzerland [*marginal note*: 'M. de Persigny forgets that Lord John Russell first proposed to the Four Powers to come to an understanding between themselves, both without us, and against us']: that he considered it necessary that some territory should be given to Switzerland, but that as he could not express himself more definitely in writing, he would call on me at three o'clock on Monday, if I had no objection. I answered that I had no instructions on the subject, but that I would see him in company with M. de la Rive, and that as I was soon leaving for Paris, I would myself impart the upshot of his remarks orally to my Government [*marginal note*: 'It is of course the only thing to do'].

"I should feel obliged if you would let me have a telegram on the subject.

"P.S. You would oblige me by communicating these remarks to the Emperor."

Was this accomplished? Here again we are left in the dark. In any case, nothing was done in the matter. By this time Persigny had himself drawn the only possible conclusion from the fundamental divergence between himself and Thouvenel. "As a matter of fact", he wrote, "there is nothing further I can do here. I am only in the way. I have outlived the broken Alliance and it is better for me to disappear."

The rest of his correspondence is of no importance.

8. Gambetta and England

by

J. P. T. BURY

THIS paper announces no discovery of new documents and proffers no revolutionary theories concerning French politics. But, so far as I am aware, it attempts something which has not been done before, and for that reason, if for no other, it may have a certain interest. My task is simply this: to consider as a whole the relations of Gambetta with England and more particularly to determine the place that country held in Gambetta's foreign policy.

The question what policy did Gambetta pursue towards England at once provokes others: What did that exuberant southerner know of our northern isles? What picture did the name England evoke? What were the sources from which he derived his knowledge of English men and manners?

The evidence is not superabundant, but it is enough to permit of answers which, I think, will not be too inexact. Gambetta drew his knowledge of England from three main sources: his reading, a visit to England, and personal contact with Englishmen whom he met in France. First of all let us consider his reading, for it was from his reading that Gambetta formed his earliest impressions of England, and, furthermore, much more is discoverable about the reading of Gambetta the student and barrister than about the reading of Gambetta the statesman. "Gambetta", recorded Joseph Reinach, "read widely, easily and quickly" and "for a long time used to take notes as he read. Later, too busy a man, he had to give up this excellent habit."[1]

[1] J. Reinach, *La Vie de Gambetta.*

In consequence the evidence as to his later reading is more scanty, and it is probable not only that he ceased to annotate his books but that the books which he had the leisure to read were in comparison less numerous.

Among the notes on his early reading in the years before 1870 are several relating to matters or persons English: a résumé of Charles de Rémusat's study of Pitt and English policy, with certain articles in the *Revue des Deux Mondes* and Sir George Lewis' *Essays on the administration of Great Britain from 1783 to 1830*" mentioned as sources; various quotations, for instance an extract from a speech delivered by Huskisson in favour of free trade; a passage from Dupin on damages, in which the words "We ought to follow the English usage on this point" are underlined; and the dictum of John Stuart Mill that "the only freedom which deserves the name, is that of pursuing our own good in our own way, so long as we do not attempt to deprive others of theirs, or impede their efforts to obtain it". Later, in an outline sketch of the workings of finance, he borrows Adam Smith's definition of taxation and refers to Ricardo, MacCulloch and James Mill. On another occasion he culls several lines of Burns and Cowper from an article by Taine, notes a phrase of Wordsworth about the rising tide of liberty sweeping away reactionary kings and writes "Admirable!" against an unremarkable line of Shelley. Elsewhere there are notes on an article about Herbert Spencer, on an analysis of Buckle's *History of Civilisation in England* and on a criticism of John Stuart Mill by Littré. Finally, there is a fairly detailed inquiry into "the political constitution of England, her administration and financial organization and the rights with which she has invested her citizens". "Grand Jury, Writ of Habeas Corpus, Docks, Clearing House"—these are some of the headings, and at the end there is a note on the system of Church patronage: "(What feudalism!)" exclaims Gambetta. But his personal opinions emerge more clearly in the comments scribbled in the margins of a copy of Prévost-Paradol's *La France Nouvelle*. For instance, Paradol writes that society in the United States was from the outset what it would have been in England if the English aristocracy had been overcome and destroyed, and what no doubt it will be there one day, once that great transformation of English society is slowly carried through. Gambetta the young Republican remarks: "In 1868 'slowly' is incorrect and short-sighted". When Paradol declares that the current which is carrying English society towards democracy is so smooth and gentle as to be almost imperceptible, Gambetta underlines "so gentle" and exclaims: "What a page could be written about the horrors of British society!" (la société britannique).

From all this there emerges the picture of an aristocratic, even feudal, country, which nevertheless possessed some useful institutions, which had had the good fortune to produce poets capable of appreciating the French Revolution and thinkers sympathetic to positivism; better still, a country which was moving rapidly towards the Elysian fields of democracy. It is indeed evident, first, that Gambetta is above all concerned to note the things which meet with his own approval, and secondly, that he is all the time seeing England through French glasses. The occasional note of an English book title or of isolated words such as "docks" and "clearing-house" is no proof of an ability to read English, and I have found no evidence to suggest that he had any first-hand acquaintance with English literature. His impressions are derived from the lectures of French professors and from articles in French reviews, especially the *Revue des Deux Mondes*. In effect, while the leader of the irreconcilables in the Parliamentary opposition of 1870 was not wholly ignorant of England, he was little concerned with her. While internal politics were ever more engrossing for a French Republican, the England of Gladstone tended to hold ever more aloof from the entanglements of continental diplomacy, and in the correspondence of Gambetta published by M. Gheusi there is no allusion of importance to England or to any Englishman.

Gambetta's knowledge of this country cannot have been vastly increased by his only visit to England. Although he travelled frequently during the last fifteen years of his life and spent many holidays in Germany, Switzerland and Italy, England never saw him then. The occasion on which he crossed the Channel was one of his first journeys abroad, but the visit was so brief that it would scarcely deserve mention had it not formed one of the most obscure and disputable episodes in his early career. It was in 1865 that he and Clément Laurier travelled to England together; and, strange to say, their object was not to make contact with English democrats but to confer with French Royalists and negotiate with Orléans princes at Twickenham. Many years later Gambetta told Dilke of his only visit to England. "That was on a curious mission", noted Dilke in August 1876, "for he came under the Empire as the representative of the Republicans to enter into consultation with the Orléans princes for the overthrow of Louis Napoleon."[1] This is not the place to examine the questions which these words of Dilke provoke, but it is interesting to note that the report that Gambetta had visited Twickenham caused some stir in Republican circles. Even as late as 1869 it was recalled and Gambetta was accused of Orleanism at an election meeting. He parried the

[1] G[wynn] and T[uckwell], *Life of* [*Sir Charles*] *Dilke*, 1, 434.

thrust with skill and good humour: "Yes, it is true, I was invited to dine with the Comte de Paris, but owing to circumstances beyond my control I did not do so. I regret it.... (Loud exclamations. Signs of general astonishment. Why?). Why, citizens? I will tell you: because the cooking there ought to be excellent!" "The audience", in the words of M. Robert Dreyfus, "explodes with merriment. What a bon vivant! The attack is repulsed."[1] Nevertheless, in spite of the repulse, the legend persisted, and in 1870 an English resident in Paris could still write: "Gambetta is very Orleanist. (That I have long heard)".[2] Such was apparently the chief positive result of the only visit Gambetta ever paid to England.

But a second visit was soon to be urged upon him in very different circumstances, and though nothing came of it those circumstances are worth recording. The time was January 1871, when a conference to discuss the revision of the Black Sea clauses of the treaty of Paris was summoned to meet in London. Paris was being bombarded and the national defence was growing desperate. Jules Favre had been named the French representative at the conference but he obstinately refused to leave the capital so long as the bombardment continued. Gambetta spent all his epistolary eloquence in the effort to persuade him, but in vain, and at length, on 27 January, he wrote that, since Favre so persistently refused, Chaudordy and the members of the Delegation at Bordeaux were urgent that he, Gambetta, would be well advised "to spend a few days in London in order to reap the fruits in the interest of our country.

---

[1] R. Dreyfus, "Les premières armes de Gambetta" (in *Revue de France*, 1 January 1933).

[2] Felix Whitehurst, *My private diary during the siege of Paris*, 10 September 1870.

But", he added, "in the midst of the difficulties which are about to press upon us it seems almost illusory for me to think of such a journey, though I still hope to see you undertake it".[1] Illusory indeed, for when Gambetta penned his despatch Favre was already at Versailles negotiating the armistice. None the less it is interesting to speculate on the rôle Gambetta might have played at this international conference. What fruits could he have reaped? Would the "subtle Genoese" have succeeded like the Piedmontese Cavour? Whatever the answer, it is highly probable that the English public would have given him a great reception. To-day Gambetta is a forgotten statesman, a name scarcely known in England, but there can have been few then to whom his name was not familiar and English opinion, hostile at the beginning of the war, was definitely veering towards sympathy with France. He would have met with a warm welcome and his presence in London might have been highly embarrassing to Gladstone and his Cabinet as well as to the German diplomatists.

It was not until after the proclamation of the Republic and, more especially, after the war, that the third source of Gambetta's knowledge of England, his contact with English visitors to France, was of any importance. One of the earliest of these contacts was also the most fruitful. In the last days of the national defence Gambetta went by sea to try and raise the flagging spirits of the northern departments, cut off by invasion from direct communication with the rest of the country. Among the audience who heard him deliver a stirring speech at Lille was a young Englishman whom he impressed immensely by his eloquence. Some months later they met and a warm friendship began: "Gambetta", wrote Sir Charles

---

[1] *Enquête parlementaire sur les actes du gouvernement de la défense nationale: Dépêches télégraphiques*, II, 477.

Dilke, "for a long time was my most intimate friend."[1] On his frequent visits to France Dilke never missed an opportunity of seeing Gambetta. "It was...Gambetta, I think, that saved me", he wrote after the death of his wife in 1874.[2] It was through Dilke that Gambetta met John Morley, Lord Randolph Churchill and Sir William Harcourt.[3] It was Dilke who later prepared the way for his introduction to the Prince of Wales. The personal friendship of two statesmen of different nations can scarcely fail to have a certain political significance; at the least it is likely to induce a juster appreciation of the national character of the peoples concerned, to make easier the avoidance of friction and to encourage a policy of mutual tolerance, if not a definite entente. So the friendship between Gambetta and Dilke had a real importance, and it was that, much more than Gambetta's visit to England and more than all his reading, which helped him to some understanding and appreciation of this country.[4]

Having thus very briefly reviewed the sources from which Gambetta drew his knowledge of England, let us pass on to some consideration of his policy. As we have seen, there is nothing in his correspondence or his conduct during the Empire to suggest that he was violently prejudiced either in favour of or against the

[1] G. and T., *Life of Dilke*, I, 153–4. [2] *Ibid.* I, 182.

[3] An amusing reference to the meeting with Lord Randolph Churchill was lately published in *The Times*, 2 July 1934: *From the Esher Papers*, VI.

[4] I confess that there is a fourth source which I have not yet had the leisure or opportunity to explore but which might well repay exploration. To the English visitors to France should be added the French visitors to England, the friends of Gambetta who crossed the Channel, correspondents of the *République Française* and personal agents sent to seek information and to act as intermediaries between him and Dilke, men such as Gérard, Henri Hecht and M. Camille Barrère. If their correspondence from England with Gambetta still exists and were visible it would almost certainly shed new light upon Gambetta's attitude towards England and upon his English policy.

English. It was the war and his sudden accession to power which abruptly compelled him to consider England as an European force, to enter into diplomatic relations with her and to seek her support. His relations with Lord Lyons, the English Ambassador, were courteous enough, but Republican diplomacy was powerless to stir the Gladstone Government from its neutrality. Nevertheless there was a decided change in English public opinion and it is possible that, when Gambetta launched his last eloquent appeals for the continuation of war to the knife, when he boldly declared that France would go on fighting for months, nay for years if necessary, he really hoped that that change would force the English Government to intervene in favour of France. But Gambetta's war policy was rejected, and the struggle ended without any practical demonstration of support for France on the part of England. Birmingham may have harvested profits but England did not win prestige from the inactivity of her rulers. She was equally unpopular alike in France and in Germany, and from Mme Adam's memoirs it is clear that Gambetta shared the feelings of the majority of his compatriots with regard to her, that he reproached the English on account of their timid isolation and of their "cowardice" in 1870.[1]

But with him the feeling did not become a profound resentment such as was to be harboured by Juliette Adam. In foreign policy hatred is a luxury and Gambetta wisely sought to limit his expenses. It was foreign policy, however, the position of France in the new post-war Europe and the question of her recovery, which were an ever increasing source of interest and preoccupation. In his correspondence we see him considering these problems from several aspects; indeed he surprises us by expressing opinions and devising combi-

[1] J. Adam, *Nos amitiés politiques* [*avant l'abandon de la revanche*], p. 390.

nations which appear quite incompatible. But here two things must be borne in mind: first, that Gambetta was always Gambetta, that is, the impulsive southerner apt to write under the impression of the moment; and secondly, that he was in power for only 73 days towards the end of his career; definitely in opposition until 1877 he was not bound by the fetters of office and the responsibilities of government, opportunist flexibility was easier.

When Gambetta returned to political life in 1871 after his temporary eclipse in Spain the foreign policy of his party could be summed up in the one word "revenge". Revenge was indeed an appropriate cry for the hero of the national defence, the man who had protested against the annexation of Alsace and Lorraine. But how was it to be obtained? Alone France durst not think of it; she was far too conscious of her own weakness and of the victor's strength, and Gambetta was as aware as anyone of the disparity. What then was to be the remedy? A policy of alliances? That coalition the very notion of which was nightmare to Bismarck? Perhaps, but Gambetta's friends were by no means agreed as to which powers were France's true allies, and whilst all the efforts of Thiers and his successors were directed to secure the "liberation of the territory" and to avoid giving offence to her powerful neighbour, Bismarck was not idle and strained every nerve to avert the danger of "Einkreisung". "Everywhere", wrote Gambetta on 4 September 1874, "he has sought and found supporters, allies and accomplices. At Vienna, Rome, Berne, St Petersburg, Washington, Madrid he is hemming us in with his diplomatic siege-works." [1] Was it an accident?— the only big Western capital which he omitted from the list was London While Mme Adam, Spuller and Ranc

[1] J. Adam, *Nos amitiés politiques*, p. 149.

were eager for alliance with Russia, Gambetta had a new English friend, Dilke, and his former Under-Secretary for Foreign Affairs at Tours, with whom he still kept in touch, was a warm partisan of entente with England. M. de Chaudordy was a diplomat by profession and Gambetta, the improviser of 1870, did not always scorn the experts' advice.

But for the moment he hesitated and allowed himself to be drawn by both sides without deciding for either. He preferred a plan of his own and still dreamed of detaching Austria, the victim of Sadowa, from the German wake: "A Franco-Austrian alliance would perhaps avert war and would in any case be the only means of making effective opposition to Prussia's lust of conquest".[1] But in the following year, 1875, when there was a real danger of war, it was not Austria but Russia and England who came to the rescue. Gambetta revised his opinion and turned towards these two powers. In a particularly interesting letter to Ranc he shook off his democratic prejudices against the Russia of the Tsars, preached a Triple Entente and for the first time quoted the opinions of the Prince of Wales: "Russia's political dreams are going to be upset by Austria who is taking up a hostile attitude. This influences Roumania. As a result do you see Austria allied with Roumania and Turkey against Russia? What a conflict! Yet the Prince of Wales foresees it. He does not share the hostile feelings of part of the English nation towards Russia. With all his youthful authority he opposes the application of measures which might be prejudicial to her. I feel that he has the makings of a great statesman....I wish Russia's enemies to be our enemies. It is clear that Bismarck wants an Austrian alliance. So Russia must perceive that we might be her allies. Before long I see

[1] P. Deschanel, *Gambetta*, p. 197.

that we shall have Russia and England with us provided we follow a reasonable policy at home".[1] To be sure Gambetta did not lack insight, but he was still undecided and, whilst in his letters to Ranc he frequently wrote in favour of a Russian alliance, at other moments he spoke in quite a different tone. Thus in the autumn of 1875, after a tour in Germany which evidently left him impressed with the power of the great enemy, he wrote to Mme Adam: "The most reckless think of a Russian alliance for France; a few others suggest an alliance with Austria and England, as though the three of us could resist the two northern courts. Happily there exists another party to which I belong and which is far from sharing such views"; and, after examining Bismarck's policy·and concluding that the Chancellor was waiting until he could bring about a collision between Russia and England or Austria, he decided that France must stand aside, avoid all commitments and let Germany work her will: "This policy may be understood in Berlin. It certainly is in London and Rome".[2] But if Germany was overwhelmingly strong France was rapidly recovering strength, and in January 1876 Gambetta was insisting that the enemy must be ringed round by an armoured wall: "Nothing need be asked of egoistic England except the protection of Belgian neutrality, but it is probable that the revival of the Polish question would suffice to carry all parties on the other side of the Channel".[3] (If this were so, would the epithet "egoistic" still be deserved?) His ideas were grandiose now and he wished to bring everyone into his encirclement project: while he told Ranc that to follow Russia and Roumania was

[1] P. Deschanel, *Gambetta*, p. 198. Gambetta did not meet the Prince of Wales until 1878 ([Sir Sidney] Lee, [*King*] *Edward VII*, 1, 162). Presumably Dilke was his present authority for the prince's opinions.
[2] J. Adam, *Nos amitiés politiques*, p. 390.
[3] *Ibid.* p. 441.

henceforth of capital interest,[1] not two months before he was still advocating alliance with Austria to Mme Adam; another year and an association of all the Latin races was his dream.[2] The contradictions are flagrant! If the data existed it would be of some interest to make a detailed analysis of the circumstances under which Gambetta wrote these letters which express so many varying views.

However, in spite of his hesitations and the obvious inconsequence of his opinions, there are some almost constant points on the European horizon as he sees it. The first is Germany. I will refrain from any discussion of the vexed question of the "abandonment of revenge" and content myself with reference to a despatch of Lord Lyons, who was well aware of the proposals for Franco-German rapprochement and of the plans for a meeting between Gambetta and Bismarck. The despatch is dated 3 January 1882, that is to say during Gambetta's brief premiership. Lyons inquires what are the motives of Gambetta's policy and comes to the conclusion that there is no reason to suppose that the so-called colonial policy was the one which Gambetta would have adopted of his own free choice. At bottom he certainly wished to obtain the recovery of France's lost provinces, but he knew very well that both the weakness of the French army and the state of public opinion would prevent any attempt to regain them for a long time to come. In the meantime Gambetta wished to free France from the kind of occult control which Germany had exercised over her, and so to improve her position and to make her once more one of the great powers of Europe.[3] In this

---

[1] 20 March 1876. P. Deschanel, *Gambetta*, p. 199.

[2] *Ibid.* p. 200.

[3] [Public Record Office], F[oreign] O[ffice], 146/2448. From Lyons, 3 January 1882. The despatch is paraphrased in [Lord] Newton, [*Life of*] *Lord Lyons*, p. 455. (Nelson's Library edition.)

paper on the relations of Gambetta and England I quote this as an English opinion and as the opinion of the man who of all Englishmen, with the possible exception of Dilke, was in the best position to form a sound judgment upon this question. In one way or another, then, Germany was still the power against whom it was always necessary to be on guard. Germany was the enemy of the future as she had been the enemy of the past, no matter how distant might be "der Tag".

The other point which remained more or less constant was England. Not that this country still clung to her policy of splendid isolation. Far from it; under a new Conservative government she showed her intention of taking an active part in the affairs of the Continent and speedily made her influence felt. Gambetta was well pleased; an entente with this new and vigorous England would be much more valuable. Though on occasion he might call her "cowardly" or "egoistic" and though his paper, the *République Française*, could be outspoken enough in its criticisms of English policy, Gambetta never agreed with Mme Adam that "perfidious Albion" (as she invariably called her) was no less than Germany France's natural enemy. And while Mme Adam pleaded passionately for an alliance with Russia, Gambetta was becoming intimate with the now anti-Russian Thiers and inclining rather to the opinion of Chaudordy, who believed that English support was essential to French recovery. "One day", declared Chaudordy in November 1877 with considerable prescience, "England will be unable to tolerate German predominance in Europe and that day there will be the opportunity for a fine stroke of policy."[1] Of course the ideal for Gambetta would have been a Triple Entente, but an Anglo-Russian seemed as remote and improbable as an Austro-Russian

[1] J. Adam, *Après l'abandon de la revanche*, p. 87.

Entente, for, as a result of events in the East, English opinion was now decidedly hostile to Russia. Bismarck would soon have to make his choice between Russia and Austria; in the same way it appeared that the French statesman in search of an ally must choose between Russia and England.

By now, and especially since 1877, Gambetta had attained a position of vast influence in France. Few were the questions of foreign policy on which he was not consulted. His influence upon Waddington's policy is disputable and Waddington himself naturally wished to minimize it,[1] but at all events, if he did direct that policy, he did so prudently. He was careful to leave all doors open and to avoid giving offence to any of the great powers. Nevertheless, if the choice had to be made between England and Russia, it is clear that he personally favoured England. In spite of momentary indignation at the Convention of 4 June 1878, which established the English in occupation of Cyprus,[2] his references to this country were usually cordial, and in the *République Française* of 7 July he defined his attitude to her with significant clarity and warmth: "A result no less important [Gambetta is discussing the consequences and achievements of the Congress of Berlin] and upon which France cannot but congratulate herself is the change in the policy of England.... England has broken away from what I would term her insular policy to renew her tradition of a continental policy.... England has made a brilliant re-entry into the European concert. Everything which happens in Europe directly affects her, for she has interests wherever political stability and civilization are at stake.

"Thus France has every reason to welcome this change

[1] See e.g. F.O. 146/2154, 13 October 1879, Adams to Salisbury.
[2] F.O. 146/2060, 10 July 1878, Lyons to Salisbury.

with delight. In effect things have resumed their logical, natural course. The interests of France and England, the two most liberal, most industrious, most productive and most wealthy countries of Europe, are so closely bound up together that the return of England to a less narrow policy brings both states at once out of the temporary isolation in which they were situated".

And still better to explain the position he added: "A Franco-Russian alliance, resting on an arbitrary basis, is no longer possible; the new state of affairs impels us naturally towards a reasoned policy, a policy of defence and of good results for all without danger for any one".

This article constituted a part of the breviary of Gambetta's policy during the last four years of his life. Noteworthy first of all is the opposition between the liberal states of France and England and a Franco-Russian alliance resting on an arbitrary basis. In spite of the suggestion of such an alliance in conversation with the Prince of Wales the next year,[1] and in spite of a natural desire to see England and Russia come to an agreement upon Eastern affairs,[2] it would seem that Gambetta no longer had much hope or confidence in Russia. He was very anti-Russian according to Dilke. "Russia is lost", he exclaimed in April 1881 soon after the assassination of Alexander II, "they are madmen."[3] Secondly, it is to be remembered that it was in 1878 that he first met the prince in whom he professed to have detected a great statesman, to wit the Prince of Wales. The two men at once took to each other, and such a friendship made its impression on the champion of "les couches nouvelles". "Gambetta has been talking to me at length about the Prince of Wales", noted Mme Adam.

[1] Lee, *Edward VII*, 1, 452.
[2] Newton, *Lord Lyons*, p. 420.
[3] L. Halévy, *Trois dîners avec Gambetta*.

"He declares that he is not a mere reveller. European and world politics interest him as much as they interest you and me, Gambetta told me, and I assure you that time is not wasted in talking to him even at a merry supper in the Café Anglais. He loves France both gaily and seriously and his dream for the future is an entente with us."[1] After the first encounter they met several times and their intimacy was on occasion of real value in soothing irritation and mitigating friction between the two countries.[2] At the prince's request Gambetta sent him his photograph; he inscribed it: "Au plus aimable des princes, un ami de l'Angleterre".[3] Further, the prince invited him to visit him in England,[4] and in 1879 Gambetta seriously thought of doing so. He would go to England, Lord Lyons explained, "not with a view to putting himself in the hands of Sir Charles Dilke and taking part in any ultra-Radical demonstration, but rather with the desire of conciliating the moderate public opinion in England, and showing that he has no desire to promote a Republican Propaganda abroad. He seems to have a decidedly friendly feeling towards the present English Ministry".[5] Lords Salisbury and Beaconsfield conveyed the assurance that they would be very happy to see him and it remained only for Gambetta to fix the date for his visit; but before he could do so the Conservatives were beaten at the general elections and the English Cabinet fell. From that moment Gambetta seems to have abandoned the idea of a journey to

---

[1] J. Adam, *Après l'abandon de la revanche*, p. 146. Sir Sidney Lee, *Edward VII*, I, 362, says that 6 May was the day when Gambetta and the prince first met, but Mme Adam appears to refer the conversation just quoted to February of this year. The chronology of her memoirs is by no means always easy to follow and I suspect that it may not always be exact.

[2] E.g. over Cyprus in 1878. Lee, *Edward VII*, I, 367.

[3] G. and T., *Life of Dilke*, I, 403.

[4] Lee, *Edward VII*, I, 362.   [5] Newton, *Lord Lyons*, p. 415.

England. This draws attention to another peculiarity of his relations with this country. In spite of his republicanism and his liberal sympathies and his friendship with Dilke, he was always on much better terms with the Conservatives than with the Liberals in England. The vigorous foreign policy of Salisbury and Beaconsfield naturally had a greater appeal for a man of Gambetta's temperament, and a strong self-assertive England was all the more likely to be an effective counterpoise to a strong and arrogant Germany. Moreover, if Tsarist autocracy was hard to digest, alliance with Conservatives in a Parliamentary country like England presented little difficulty to a Republican opportunist. Finally, there was a personal element; Gambetta was not the man to love preachers and moralists: "Gladstone detests me", he said at dinner with the Marquis du Lau. "I got on splendidly with Disraeli".[1]

But Gladstone's return to power did not lessen Gambetta's desire for an entente with England and his contact with the new Cabinet was close, for Dilke was a member of the Ministry as Under-Secretary of State for Foreign Affairs. Henceforward the great question was whether one part of the Gambettist creed, the policy of expansion, the colonial policy which he was beginning to favour, could be reconciled with the policy of entente. Bismarck did not think it possible, and for that very reason encouraged France's colonial ambitions, hoping that the Anglo-French condominium in Egypt would prove a new Schleswig-Holstein. To be sure an entente was not easily obtainable, for the new French policy revived old English jealousies, and in all that concerned her maritime power and her control of the passage to India England was particularly sensitive.

[1] L. Halévy, *Trois dîners avec Gambetta*; J. Morley, *Life of Gladstone*, III, 465.

But Gambetta refused to be discouraged and in Egyptian affairs exerted every effort to maintain cordial co-operation. Finally, when he himself was in office, it was he who took the initiative and determined the despatch of the Joint Note intended to strengthen Tewfik Pasha's hand. His policy was firm, but it was fruitless, for the "grand ministère", with which he might have hoped to steer French policy for many months, was little more than a fleeting silhouette on the parliamentary scene and too bold a foreign policy was certainly not the sin of its successor. Events in Egypt followed one another in rapid succession, and the condominium crumbled owing to the hesitations of a government in which Gambetta had no part. The *République Française* was loud in its condemnation of Freycinet's weakness, and it was significant that the last great speech which Gambetta uttered in the Chamber was an eloquent plea for the maintenance of an Anglo-French Entente. I will quote one of the most striking passages of what might well be called his political testament: "Gentlemen, when I consider Europe, this Europe which has been the subject of so much discussion here to-day, I observe that during the past ten years there has always been a Western policy represented by France and England. Let me say that I know of no other European policy which could be of any assistance to us in the most terrible circumstances we could have to fear.... Well, I have seen enough to be able to say this: at the cost of the greatest sacrifices never break with the English alliance. Oh, I know what may be said. Enough of all equivocation. I will tell you everything that I have in mind. I am indeed a sincere and enlightened friend of the English, though not so much so as to sacrifice French interests to them. Besides, you may be sure that the English, good politicians that they are, esteem only those allies who know how to make themselves respected and to secure that their interests should be taken into account. (Applause on the Left and in the Centre.)

"And precisely—I am telling you everything, for I have nothing to conceal—precisely what draws me to the English alliance, to co-operation with England in the Mediterranean and in Egypt, is that what I fear most— apart that is from that calamitous rupture—is that you should abandon to England, and abandon for ever, territories and rivers and rights of way where your right to live and traffic is no less than hers.

"So it is not with the least intention of humiliating France or of lowering and weakening her interests that I am an advocate of the English alliance; it is because I believe, gentlemen, that it is only through this co-opera-tion that those interests can be effectively safeguarded."[1]

A frank, nationalist, energetic, realist, policy with a full realization of the benefits of an Entente Cordiale. But if Gambetta had remained in power could he have carried it through? It is a doubtful question. On the one hand it could be argued that he alone could have pre-served the entente at this time, and that his influence alone could have averted the dangerous friction which was to lead the two countries to the brink of war and to that rupture which he regarded as so calamitous; but on the other hand it might be maintained that, as Bismarck professed to fear, Gambetta's policy directed by Gam-betta would have led directly to an armed clash and that his determination to preserve French interests was not compatible with the preservation of the entente.

> Had his wild strength crested its highest wave?
> Would it have worked to shatter or to save?
> There comes no answer from Gambetta's grave.[2]

[1] J. Reinach, *Gambetta. Discours et plaidoyers politiques*, XI, 103–4.
[2] *Punch*, 13 January 1883.

Speculation as to the might have been is more amusing than useful and we must be content with Mr Punch's answer answerless.

In this brief outline it has been impossible for me to enter into all the details of Gambetta's policy towards England since he reached a position of commanding influence in France. I have attempted merely to sketch the main features of this policy, to suggest its development and to emphasize its continuity. To sum up, the desire for a friendly understanding with England emerges as one of the most constant points and one of the dominating ideas in the foreign policy of this founder of the Third Republic. And if Gambetta were with us here to-day would he not with burning eloquence assert that history has justified him and point to 1914 as the proof?

9. The Foreign Policy of Lord Salisbury, 1878–80. The Problem of the Ottoman Empire

by

LILLIAN PENSON

AT the end of March 1878 Lord Salisbury, who had been since 1874 a member of Disraeli's Cabinet as Secretary of State for India, succeeded Lord Derby at the Foreign Office. Salisbury was already well versed in foreign affairs, for not only had his tenure of the India Office involved diplomatic negotiations of peculiar difficulty, but as a member of the Cabinet, and in particular as British representative at the Constantinople Conference, he had taken a prominent part in the discussion of the most critical problem of the period, the question of Turkey.

The circumstances of Salisbury's transfer to the Foreign Office combine with other factors to make it peculiarly difficult to assess his policy during the period 1878–80. After the change, as well as before, the control of British policy was largely in the hands of Disraeli. Some writers indeed hold that Salisbury to a greater extent than Derby was subordinated to his chief.[1] And although this may not actually be the case, the sphere of independent judgment open to the new Foreign Secretary was undoubtedly narrow. He had, therefore, to conform to directing lines already laid down; he was hampered, in one important branch of his policy in particular, by principles enunciated before he assumed the Foreign Secretaryship. With these disadvantages he had to face the fact that for over a year the British Cabinet had been

[1] Cp. G. Hanotaux, *Histoire de la France contemporaine*, IV, 336.

moving towards a new statement of the British attitude
to the Ottoman Empire. Its character was not yet
decided. The traditional insistence on independence and
integrity was already gone. But what should take its
place? If it is true that Salisbury's achievement during
his first two years at the Foreign Office was the most
brilliant of his career—a view quoted by Lady Gwendolen Cecil as being that of Lord Rosebery[1] and endorsed
by Sir James Headlam-Morley in his study on the Cyprus
Convention[2]—it is because of his treatment of this
problem. In the few months of 1878 Salisbury mapped
out the frontiers of a policy with masterly draughtman-
ship. The details were elaborated with enforced speed,
and this hurry made mistakes inevitable. But he completed his design—and, though it did indeed fail, there
was an element of grandeur in its boldness.

Salisbury's design can be reconstructed from a study
of his treatment of the triple problem of Turkey-in-
Europe, Turkey-in-Asia and Turkey-in-Africa. With
regard to Turkey-in-Europe all that could be done in
his view was to draw a new line of defence. "The
Turkish...breakwater", he wrote, "is now shattered,...
Another dyke may have to be established behind it."[3]
This view was clearly held by the British Cabinet before
Salisbury became Secretary of State for Foreign Affairs.
It is implicit in the negotiations which Lord Derby
conducted in May and June 1877 with Count Beust, and
in his contemporary conversations with Count Schuvalov. The arrangements concluded by Salisbury with
Russia and Austria-Hungary a year later followed much
the same lines. The conversations with Count Beust

[1] *Life of Robert, Marquis of Salisbury*, II, 231.
[2] *Studies in Diplomatic History*, p. 203.
[3] B[ritish M[useum] Add. MSS. 39137. Salisbury to Layard, Private,
4 April 1878. Cited Lady Gwendolen Cecil, *Life of Robert, Marquis of
Salisbury*, II, 264.

were renewed on 3 April 1878 with specific reference to the negotiations of the previous year.[1] In his dealings with Count Schuvalov Salisbury based his proposals for the frontiers of Bulgaria on those put forward at the Conference of Constantinople and in the subsequent Anglo-Austrian conversations.[2] In 1878 as in 1877 it is clear that the British object was to give Turkey a new lease of an area sufficient, in Salisbury's words, "to protect strategically its position at Constantinople",[3] or, as he said to Count Beust, to secure that sufficient authority be left to the Porte to make it "politically independent and strategically safe".[4] Except for his desire to provide a safe military frontier and a sufficient hinterland for the protection of Constantinople, Salisbury seems to have cared little for Turkey-in-Europe. He wanted merely a settlement which would put off further disturbance as long as possible—to postpone the time when Turkey-in-Europe "must go". Hence the tenour of his negotiations on the Greek frontier question; their object was, he said, to "remove, at least for many years to come, a source of constant disturbance and disorder to the Turkish border provinces".[5] Hence his insistence, which is found in both his official despatches and his private letters, on the desirability of an Austro-Turkish convention. He wanted Austria-Hungary to undertake to protect Turkey-in-Europe against Servia and Montenegro. "It would be of the highest value to the Porte", Salisbury telegraphed from Berlin, "to secure an Austrian guarantee against attack from Servia

[1] [Public Record Office], F[oreign] O[ffice] 7/923. Salisbury to Elliot, No. 236 of 3 April 1878. Cp. for these negotiations generally, W. A. Gauld, "The Anglo-Austrian Agreement of 1878" (*English Historical Review*, XLI, January 1926).
[2] F.O. 65/994. Salisbury to Loftus, No. 334 of 24 May 1878.
[3] B.M. Add. MSS. 39137. Salisbury to Layard, 2 May 1878.
[4] F.O. 7/924. Salisbury to Elliot, No. 358 of 31 May 1878.
[5] F.O. 78/2791. Layard to Salisbury, No. 758 of 11 June 1878.

and Montenegro and if possible from Bulgaria and it would be very unwise not to take advantage of the apparent present readiness of Count Andrassy to give such a guarantee."[1] The occupation of Bosnia and Herzegovina would be the price, and on this point the negotiations broke down. Salisbury may have been misled as to the readiness of Count Andrassy, but it seems likely that the Porte could have obtained, at one time, an "official note to guarantee Turkey against attack from Servia and Montenegro" had the Porte been prepared for a previous "Convention establishing an agreement between the two Governments on the subject of the occupation".[2]

Salisbury's real concern, however, was with Turkey-in-Asia. There, as he wrote to Layard, was the true source of Turkish power. It was the "nursery of her troops". There too, Salisbury seems to have believed, Ottoman rule was at least no worse than that of any other Government that could be established, while with British help and protection it might become better. The relative importance in Salisbury's mind of Turkey-in-Europe and Turkey-in-Asia is shown clearly in a private letter to Sir Henry Layard written in August 1878:

"I have been in some doubt how to act. On the one hand I am deeply convinced of the unwisdom of the course the Porte is pursuing. Its policy is to make Austria its friend: and though I can quite understand the contention that Austria's friendship is not worth two provinces, at least when the two provinces are hopelessly gone it is worth while for the sake of the two provinces to accept the inevitable with grace and promptitude. The Porte, it is abundantly proved, is not strong enough to stand alone. It must be held up. We offer ourselves

[1] F.O. 78/2769. Salisbury to Layard, Tel. unnumbered of 19 July 1878.
[2] F.O. 7/933. Elliot to Salisbury, No. 567 of 12 August 1878.

as supporters on the East, Austria on the West. If Austria can only be bound to prevent attack from Servia or Montenegro from attacking Turkey, the latter can defend itself against any other: for Servia, held back herself will not allow Bulgaria to go in for loot alone: and Russia has no further bribes now to offer to Roumania. This convention of Guarantee, which we have earnestly urged both on Austria and Turkey, is, therefore, an integral link in the line of defence. That Greece must have a rectification I do not doubt.. . .

"But all these considerations both with respect to Austria and Greece are subordinate in my mind to the dominant object of using British influence for British purposes, i.e. for purposes which under the [Cyprus] Convention have become British. We want besides our demands as to Cyprus—which by this time I trust are satisfied—our reforms in Asia, and security for their being carried out. And assuming that the Sultan will listen the more to our demands if we do not come too often as solicitors for others, I have been chary of recommending to you any urgent action with respect to Greece, and till very lately of Austria. I only pressed strongly on account of Austria these last few days when it seemed likely that a serious renewal of disturbances in the whole peninsula might result from a continuance of the conflict."[1]

The problem of the Asiatic frontiers lay outside the sphere of the Anglo-Austrian negotiations: "The first point", wrote Salisbury to Sir Henry Elliot, "in which it appeared evident from the communications held with the Austrian Gov[ernment] that no help was to be expected from them, was in regard to the increase of Russian territory in Asia".[2] And Salisbury insisted in

[1] B.M. Add. MSS. 39138. Salisbury to Layard, 13 August 1878.
[2] F.O. 7/924. Salisbury to Elliot, No. 370 of 3 June 1878.

his conversations with Count Beust that a parallel was to be found here to the British inability to support Austro-Hungarian interests in Herzegovina. In neither case could the two Powers be of assistance to one another. Hence the importance which was given to the Asiatic problem in the Anglo-Russian arrangements of 30 and 31 May; hence the simultaneous negotiations with the Porte.

The security of Turkey-in-Asia was protected in the first place by the Salisbury-Schuvalov agreement of 31 May, under which Russia gave a specific undertaking "not to extend her conquests in Asia beyond Kars, Batum and the limits laid down by the Preliminary Treaty of San Stefano", as modified by the terms of the memorandum of 30 May, that is, by the restitution of the valley of Alashkert and the town of Bayazid.[1] The engagement was even more secret than the memorandum of the previous day. Count Schuvalov stipulated that it should not be published without Russian consent even if the earlier document became public. In the event it escaped the betrayal of the other documents to the *Globe*, and Russia refused consent to its inclusion in the proposed Parliamentary Paper of August 1878. The Russian refusal was based, comprehensibly enough, on the distrust involved in the simultaneous negotiation of the Cyprus Convention. The rather specious explanation, that the Cyprus Convention was "a supplement to" the Russian engagement and founded upon it, failed to convince Gorchakov.[2] It might, in fact, be credible, had the Convention stood alone, but it becomes wholly impossible of acceptance in the light of Salisbury's attempt to change the rule of the Straits. Both the Cyprus Convention and the proposals regarding the

[1] F.O. 65/1022.
[2] F.O. 65/1005. Loftus to Salisbury, No. 656 of 20 July 1878.

Straits were conditional on the Russian retention of conquests in Asia. The avowed object of the Straits proposal was to force Russia to make concessions, or if this failed to "make good the only weak place in our policy", that is, "to counteract the disturbance of the balance of power in the Black Sea".[1] The change in the rule of the Straits and the occupation of Cyprus were two parts of one policy—the defence of Asia.

There is little evidence as to Salisbury's share in the decision to occupy Cyprus.[2] The evidence, however, is ample as to the interpretation he placed on the alliance of which the occupation was the symbol. There is comparatively little, in Salisbury's correspondence, of Cyprus as a "place of arms". Layard, it is true, was instructed both in a private telegram of 24 May and in the despatch of the same date to speak of it to the Porte as necessary for the defence of Asia. "It is impossible for England to exercise the necessary vigilance over Syria and Asia Minor and to accumulate when required troops and material of war in time to be of use in repelling invasions or frustrating foreign attempts to rebellion in Asia Minor or Syria, unless she possesses a stronghold near the coast."[3] But this was the language of negotiation. From the many letters written before and after this date it is clear that Cyprus was not so much a place of arms as a symbol and an opportunity. It was a symbol to Russia and the peoples of Asia Minor of Britain's determination to defend her interests. "The mere presence of the Russians at Kars will cause Persia,

---

[1] F.O. 78/2911. Memorandum for the Cabinet [regarding the Straits].
[2] For the question of the Cyprus Convention generally, v. Sir James Headlam-Morley's article, cited above; Professor H. Temperley, "Disraeli and Cyprus", *English Historical Review*, XLVI, April and July 1931; Professor Dwight E. Lee, "A Memorandum concerning Cyprus, 1878", *Journal of Modern History*, III, June 1931.
[3] B.M. Add. MSS. 39137. Salisbury to Layard, Tel. of 24 May 1878.

Mesopotamia, Syria, to turn their faces Northward. Then a Russian party will arise—and consequent disorder —and the languid administrative powers of the Porte will be overtaxed—and a chaos will follow of which in some form or other the Russians will take advantage.... The presence of England is the only remedy which can prevent this process of destruction from going forward."[1] It was a symbol, too, to the British electorate, to whom the defence of Asia would not necessarily appeal as it did to a Prime Minister who had purchased the Suez Canal shares or to a Foreign Secretary who had had two terms of service at the India Office. "This country", Salisbury said, "which is popularly governed, and cannot therefore be counted on to act on any uniform or consistent system of policy would probably abandon the task of resisting any further Russian advance...if no other but speculative arguments can be advanced in favour of action. But it will cling to any military port occupied by England as tenaciously as it has clung to Gibraltar."[2] Cyprus was thus a concrete object to which British public opinion could be rallied if the issue were again one of peace or war.

The Convention was, moreover, an opportunity. It gave Great Britain a locality in which to make improvements in administration, and, though proof is lacking, this may well have been the decisive factor in the choice of Cyprus as the pledge of the Convention. Layard, whose prevision was far greater than that of Salisbury, had pressed for Mohammerah or some other station on the Persian Gulf, alleging its greater usefulness both for defence and trade. His second choice was for a port

[1] B.M. Add. MSS. 39137. Salisbury to Layard, 2 May 1878. (Cited by Lady Gwendolen Cecil, II, 266.)

[2] B.M. Add. MSS. 39137. Salisbury to Layard, 18 April 1878. (Cited by Professor Temperley in his article on "Disraeli and Cyprus", *English Historical Review*, April 1931.)

on the northern part of the Syrian coast, "which would command the terminus of the railway which might ultimately be carried from the Mediterranean through the valley of the Euphrates or of the Tigris to the Persian Gulf". Yet Layard, while he thought Cyprus less important strategically, recognized its value as affording "an example of the effects of good government and of a well-ordered administration".[1] The importance of this object is emphasized also in Colonel Home's memorandum,[2] which bears a minute claiming that "it was upon this paper that the Convention...had been agreed". The difficulty in dating this document detracts greatly from its value as evidence, but the principle governing it—that the political considerations were more important than the strategic—is fully in accord with the trend of Salisbury's correspondence. Cyprus was a place where "good government will quickly produce results....What is done in Cyprus will be known all through Syria and Asia Minor". The Convention as a whole, however, did more. Reform in Cyprus was to be a model for reform elsewhere, and the Convention gave Britain a *locus standi* in more senses than one. Salisbury knew well that without reforms the whole of his scheme would fail. A new Gladstone might appear to popularize a new "atrocities" campaign—and against this the most skilful diplomacy would be useless. "This Convention", he wrote to Layard on 17 July, "will give you a strong plea for pressing your advice."[3] A week later an official despatch reiterated these views. The "necessary reforms in Asia" were described

---

[1] B.M. Add. MSS. 38937. Layard Memoirs, ff. 82, 104.

[2] F.O. 358/1. Cp. Professor Temperley's article, "Further evidence on Disraeli and Cyprus", *English Historical Review*, XLVI, July 1931; Professor Dwight E. Lee, "A Memorandum concerning Cyprus, 1878", *Journal of Modern History*, III June 1931.

[3] B.M. Add. MSS. 39138. Salisbury to Layard, 17 July 1878.

as "the first object of Her Majesty's Government", and to the securing of this and a settlement of questions relating to Cyprus all other objects were to be subordinated.

The character of the reforms which Salisbury desired to introduce into Turkey-in-Asia was the subject of considerable correspondence, both official and private, with Sir Henry Layard. The object of the reforms according to Salisbury was twofold—to "remove all pretext for disaffection, and...strengthen the Ottoman Monarchy". The method was suggested at the same time—"Good Government in Asia means Government by good men: and the whole problem is—to find these good men and keep them.... It is in your power to judge, from what passes on the spot, who the good men are: or at least who are the least bad". It is clear from the correspondence that Salisbury from the beginning thought that to secure "good men" it was necessary that they should be Europeans, and while he thought that it would be impossible to secure the appointment of European Governors he welcomed Sir Henry Layard's proposal "for attaching to each Vali a European ad latus", and held moreover that European officers for the Gendarmerie were essential.[1] The chief branches of reform which Layard was to press upon the Porte were discussed in detail in a Cabinet meeting on 7 August on the basis of a despatch which was sent to Layard on the 8th. A private letter supplemented the despatch and contained, as the more formal document did not, a reference to the British advisers "whom it has been proposed to put near the Governor". The omission was made, Salisbury said, deliberately, "because the despatch may possibly be published:[2] and these English

[1] B.M. Add. MSS. 39138. Salisbury to Layard, 17 and 24 July 1878.
[2] It was in fact published in *Accounts and Papers*, 1879, LXXIX (C. 2202), 11–14.

Advisers may seem to resemble superficially the Resident of an Indian Native Court so closely, that the discussion of their attributions would almost inevitably contain matter offensive both to the Turk and Foreign Powers ".[1] As the correspondence continues it becomes clear that Salisbury realized that his scheme was bound to fail. He was unable "for constitutional reasons", as he put it, to guarantee the loan for which the Sultan asked; the House of Commons showed its attitude clearly on this matter, in December, when the Government "put out a pilot balloon".[2] In October 1878 the Sultan made promises for reform in Asia which went far to meet British views—European Inspectors for the Gendarmerie and for the Judicial Tribunals, European Financial Inspectors for the Vilayets;[3] but they were still lacking a year after the promises had been made.[4] The appointment of Lieutenant-Colonel Wilson in April 1879 as Consul-General in Anatolia, with instructions referring specifically to the Convention of 4 June,[5] was made abortive to a large extent by the attitude of the Porte. The work of General Baker, who was appointed in the following November Inspector-General of Reforms in Asia Minor, was similarly hampered. Three months after he started work he reported that he was still unable to get "any definite basis for the organisation of the Gendarmerie. The provisional reorganisation sent out some five months ago is a mere sham".[6] Sir Henry Layard commented bitterly on the difficulties made by the Porte over the appointment of

[1] B.M. Add. MSS. 39138. Salisbury to Layard, 7 August 1878.
[2] Cp. Lady Gwendolen Cecil, II, 313–14.
[3] F.O. 78/2803. Safvet Pasha to Sir H. Layard, 24 October 1878. Enclosure in Despatch No. 1319 of 24 October 1878.
[4] F.O. 78/2960. Layard to Salisbury, No. 929 of 29 October 1879.
[5] F.O. 78/2987. Salisbury to Colonel Wilson, No. 1 of 24 April 1879.
[6] F.O. 78/3081. Baker Pasha to Sir Henry Layard, 1 February 1880. Enclosure in Sir Henry Layard's Despatch No. 235 of 24 February 1880.

Colonel Cope and Colonel Norton as Inspectors of Gendarmerie at Bitlis and Erzerum at the beginning of 1880; they were "merely sent on their present missions in order to enable the Porte to say that they are employed".[1] As regards the Judicial Inspectors the fault does not seem to be wholly on the side of the Porte. Salisbury failed to realize his dream of a service organized on the model of that of India, and the terms offered by Turkey were insufficient to attract the only Englishman who was, in Sir Henry Layard's view, suitable for the post. Similar difficulties hindered the appointment of a French financial adviser and British officials to assist in the Customs House administration.

Reform in Turkey-in-Asia was one side of Salisbury's policy and one aspect of his aim to avoid the growth of Russian influence. On the other side was the problem of defence. And if the occupation of Cyprus was in his view rather a symbol and an opportunity than an instrument of defence, it would have been inconsistent with the principles on which he worked if no other step had been taken to make possible the fulfilment of the new British obligation to defend Turkey-in-Asia. This is the place in his policy of the alteration in the rule of the Straits. Salisbury would have preferred that the Straits should be open to all, and a report of a Cabinet Committee at the end of March 1878 shows that he had support for this preference. Such a complete reversal of British policy was, however, considered impracticable. The Porte would be certain to object. Moreover Derby in May 1877 had pronounced in favour of the maintenance of the existing system, and Count Schuvalov countered Salisbury's proposals by citing Derby's views. Salisbury therefore put forward the idea of a special agreement referring to Great Britain alone and sent a

[1] F.O. 78/3080. Layard to Salisbury, No. 132 of 28 January 1880.

draft of this privately to Sir Henry Layard in June during the Congress of Berlin. The Porte was to undertake not to offer "forcible opposition to the passage at any time of the English fleet thro[ugh] the Straits of the Dardanelles and Bosphorus" should England "be of opinion that the presence of a naval force in the Black Sea is expedient with view to protect the Sultan's interests".[1] Layard reported the next day that the "G[ran]d Vizier is disposed to consent to agreement provided it be kept very secret",[2] and Salisbury telegraphed on the 21st, "Get the agreement about Straits if you can".[3] These instructions had, however, to be cancelled, for the Cabinet at home were "with one exception" opposed to them. Salisbury had therefore still further to modify his policy. Without any specific agreement, he thought, the nature of the British obligation could be changed by a declaration at the Congress. He explained his reasons in a memorandum sent home from Berlin for the approval of the Cabinet.[4] "It will...make the control over the Straits a real control, to be exercised by the Turkish Government itself—and not by another Government standing behind it. The Sultan now, to defend himself, has to summon his allies formally: an act of defiance to Russia he may well be too panic struck to take. If the policy we propose be adopted, he will only have to utter the much easier and safer words, 'I am too weak to resist England'. We...shall simply be in the position of dispensing with the formal summons of a friend who is under duress." The Cabinet approval of this project is shown by the "Cabinet alterations" on the draft declaration for Congress which accompanied the memorandum; alterations which strengthen rather than diminish the force of the

---

[1] B.M. Add. MSS. 39137. Salisbury to Layard, 16 June 1878.
[2] B.M. Add. MSS. 39137. Layard to Salisbury, 17 June 1878.
[3] B.M. Add. MSS. 39137. Salisbury to Layard, 21 June 1878.
[4] F.O. 78/2911. Memorandum for the Cabinet, June 1878.

statement. Actually, however, the declaration was not made in full. Russia undertook that Batum should be "essentially commercial" and agreed to a modification of the frontier line. The latter, however, was not sufficient to satisfy Salisbury; hence he made the declaration in substance.[1] Russia professed at the time of her counter-declaration not to understand its significance, but, if this was the case, her confusion was short-lived. It is given an important place in the memorandum which Saburov addressed to the German Government on 5 February 1880,[2] and in the terms of the Drei-Kaiser Bund of 1881. It was one of the most ill-judged elements in Salisbury's policy, for it caused suspicion and annoyance to other Powers, without bringing any compensating advantage.

The correspondence of the period, both official and private, shows increasing fear that British influence in Turkey was declining. The maintenance of this influence, described by Salisbury in September 1878 as "one of the most important objects of British policy—perhaps the most vital of all",[3] was damaged by many factors. Salisbury recognized that the constant pressure for reforms itself constituted a danger. It made "virtue so disagreeable while vice is so very pleasant".[4] Malet, who was in charge of the Constantinople embassy for some months while Sir Henry Layard was absent, attributed the decline to several reasons. The people of Turkey-in-Asia had been disappointed that the Convention of 4 June had not led to their deliverance from misrule and oppression. The Afghan War had destroyed the view that Britain was the protector of Islam. British influence

[1] Protocol No. 18 of 11 July 1878. Cp. Hertslet, *Map of Europe by Treaty*, IV, 2727.
[2] *Grosse Politik*, III, 144–5.
[3] B.M. Add. MSS. 39138. Salisbury to Layard, 18 September 1878.
[4] B.M. Add. MSS. 39139. Salisbury to Layard, 2 January 1880.

in Egypt had failed to secure good government and thus had broken another illusion. The acquisition of Cyprus had given the impression that British zeal for the integrity of the Ottoman Empire was a sham.[1] A little later another factor became operative, with the increasing realization of the new British attitude to Tunis.

The weakness of Salisbury's policy is shown perhaps most clearly of all in this branch of his negotiations. He entered into private conversations with M. Waddington at Berlin, conversations which, as he himself stated later, took place "on steamers, in railway carriages and in ladies' drawing rooms" and were not recorded. He seems to have hoped that they might be kept secret. Yet it could hardly be expected that M. Waddington, beset as he was with the public outcry in France over the Cyprus Convention, would fail to make use of the assurances he had received. Salisbury indeed did not attempt to retract his undertaking; on the contrary he confirmed it in a despatch to Lord Lyons of 7 August[2] and in conversations with M. Waddington in September. Yet he failed to implement the change in policy which these assurances had involved. On the very day of his despatch to Lord Lyons he wrote to the British agent in Tunis denying a local rumour as to the new attitude of Britain. "I have to inform you", he wrote, "that no offer of the annexation of Tunis to France has ever been made by Her Majesty's Government to the French Government",[3] a statement no doubt literally true but liable to misinterpretation. The British agent continued in consequence his opposition to the development of French influence and ultimately paid for his misinterpretation by his recall.

[1] F.O. 78/2949. Malet to Salisbury, No. 375 of 4 May 1879.
[2] F.O. 27/2300. Salisbury to Lyons, No. 493 of 7 August 1878.
[3] F.O. 102/111. Salisbury to Wood, No. 15 of 7 August 1878.

Salisbury paid even more heavily—for his action as to Tunis was an important factor in the decline of British influence at Constantinople. There is no evidence indeed that the Porte knew of the British attitude in 1878, though M. Fournier, the French Ambassador at Constantinople, told Sir Henry Layard in October that he had seen in writing "an offer...to acquiesce in the French annexation of Tunis". In any case, however, the secret of British policy could not long be kept. The withdrawal of Consul-General Wood from Tunis in January 1879 was an acknowledgment which it would be difficult to mistake, for he had represented for a quarter of a century the Palmerstonian policy of Turkish integrity in that part of the Ottoman dominions. Moreover, as far back as August 1878 the news was rife in Tunis. As Layard said, when he repeated M. Fournier's statement, if the Porte hear of this "you will easily understand that the serious difficulties with w[hic]h I have to contend here...would be greatly increased".[1] It is significant that up to October 1878 Layard had received no information from Salisbury regarding the change in British policy—and was still under the impression that Tunis was looked upon in England as an integral part of the Ottoman Empire.

Two interpretations of Salisbury's attitude seem possible. One is that he allowed the diplomatic object of conciliating France to outrun his political aim of influencing Turkey—and for that reason he conveniently forgot at Berlin that the Ottoman Empire was the middle-kingdom not of two but of three continents. The other interpretation is, perhaps, more credible. Salisbury realized from the first that a genuine improvement in the standard of Turkish rule in all parts of the Empire was the only real defence of Turkey against her great

[1] B.M. Add. MSS. 39138. Layard to Salisbury, 18 October 1878.

European neighbours. For this a system of protection was needed. There was thus moral if not literal accuracy in the vivid language which M. Waddington attributed to him—"vous ne pouvez pas laisser Carthage aux mains des barbares".[1] Running through the whole of Salisbury's negotiations of this period is one thread. Sometimes almost invisible and undoubtedly weak, it nevertheless justifies the statement that Salisbury had a consistent design. He wanted to substitute practical and limited obligations for the "pure mockery" of the outworn Tripartite Agreement. Austria-Hungary in Europe, Britain in Asia Minor, France in Tunis, represented three aspects of one policy. The protection of the Ottoman Empire, a "protection" on the Indian model, was Salisbury's new watchword in the place of "independence and integrity".

Salisbury fell in the spring of 1880 and was succeeded by ministers to whom "Disraeli's new Malta" and Salisbury's promises as to Tunis were alike abhorrent. Both had to be maintained—but the design which they had represented fell to pieces. The new ministers laid before Parliament in 1881 the despatches regarding Tunis which Salisbury had so carefully kept secret.[2] They entered upon a course of policy in Egypt which further diminished British influence at Constantinople, and as a result of both these actions they helped to bring about the Triple Alliance, just as Salisbury's declaration regarding the Straits contributed to the formation of the Drei-Kaiser Bund. A few years later Lord Rosebery lost his opportunity to make good the Straits declaration— in 1886 when Russia altered the status of Batum. Parliamentary changes were therefore one reason for Salisbury's failure. But it is doubtful whether in any

[1] *Documents diplomatiques français* (1871–1914), 1ère Sér. II, 367.
[2] *Accounts and Papers*, 1881, XCIX (C. 2886), 501–7.

case he could have been successful. British influence in Asia Minor was palatable to the Turk only if it brought advantages elsewhere—the guarantee of a loan, defence against Austria-Hungary as well as Russia in Europe and against France in Africa. This was far from being in accord with Salisbury's idea of protection. His practical substitute for independence and integrity was inherently unpractical. The design involved the political aim of influence at Constantinople and something more than influence in Turkey-in-Asia, both securing the ultimate object of the control of the route to the East. It involved also the diplomatic objects of maintaining peace in Turkey-in-Europe and co-operation with Austria-Hungary and France. Success could have been attained only if the Porte had been kept ignorant of the implications of Salisbury's policy, and before such a task even the most rigid precautions of secrecy must have failed.

10. The début of M. Paul Cambon in England, 1899–1903

by

PROFESSOR PAUL MANTOUX

IN the history of Franco-British relations, M. Paul Cambon's tenure of the London embassy holds an exceptional place. That authority which enabled him to play so important a part at the gravest junctures was based, above all, on the trust reposed in him—and we are aware of all that the word "trust" stands for in England. M. Cambon is remembered there chiefly for the years during which he was in possession of that unique asset. Properly to estimate its value it is necessary to recall the difficulties encountered by him at the outset of his mission to London in the late 'nineties. Therein lies the interest of the documents relating to his earliest impressions, on first coming into contact with the British Government. Pending their publication in a forthcoming volume of the *documents diplomatiques français* (1870–1914), it seemed appropriate to give a brief account of those documents so as to throw a certain amount of light on that decisive moment in a great career that marked a turning point in the history of the two countries.

I

The appointment of M. Cambon to the French embassy in London was decided upon just as the crisis brought about by the arrival at Fashoda of the Marchand Mission was entering upon its acutest stage. Marchand reached Fashoda on 10 July 1898; his famous meeting with Kitchener took place on 19 September. That very day Sir Edmund Monson informed Lord Salisbury of the nomination of M. Paul Cambon to supersede Baron de Courcel. "M. Delcassé told me", wrote the British Ambassador, "that he hoped the choice would prove acceptable to the Queen, and requested me to assure Your Lordship that the Government of the Republic, moved by a sincere desire to establish and consolidate the relations between the two countries on a basis of complete harmony, has taken into consideration the character and outlook of M. Cambon, who is known to be an earnest friend of England and the English—a fact of which Her Majesty's Government must already have been apprised by Sir Philip Currie", added the minister.[1] M. Cambon, indeed, had had more than one opportunity, in Constantinople, of collaborating with his English colleague. There was, of course, no lack of subjects of disagreement—including Egypt—in the Near East, and the attitude towards M. Cambon of the members of the British embassy with the Sublime Porte had been, at the outset, one of a none too benignant observation. "Very clever", was the verdict of Sir Arthur Nicolson—who was destined, later on, to collaborate with him so closely—"quite Monsieur le Préfet,[2] until on finding one is not intimidated, he becomes human. He is eaten up with the desire to achieve some diplomatic success. He is a most agreeable man, but I should think, a big schemer."[3] This impression, however, was amended in the course of the next few years, on account, more particularly, of the foresight and courage with which, at the time of the Armenian massacres, M. Cambon co-operated with his English colleague, to prevent a conflict between Great Britain and Russia.

[1] F.O. 3396 (No. 464). Gooch and Temperley, *British Documents*, 1, 166.

[2] M. Cambon, of course, had been a Préfet for several years, before being appointed Résident-Général in Tunis and subsequently Ambassador in Madrid.

[3] Quoted by Harold Nicolson. *Lord Carnock*, p. 91.

When he arrived in London, on 8 December 1898, the most dangerous moment of the crisis was over, as we know to-day. As far back as 4 November, Baron de Courcel had informed Lord Salisbury of the decision arrived at in Paris to recall the Marchand Mission, and had submitted to him the proposal to entrust a joint commission with the task of preparing, for the territories lying to the East of Lake Chad, a delimitation similar to that which already shared out the region of the Niger between the two rival influences. The British Prime Minister, however, would admit of no conversation so long as Marchand remained at Fashoda, and the situation remained obscure and disquieting. The French public, which had shown no great concern when British anger had been at its highest, was very disgruntled by the "climb-down" of its Government. In England, the promise to evacuate Fashoda had not immediately appeased an opinion inflamed by a campaign of the entire Press, which set forth at full length all the grievances of the Empire against French Colonial policy, especially in economic matters. In West Africa, Madagascar, New-foundland, Indo-China and the New Hebrides, France was accused of constantly renewing the "pin pricks" which, in the long run, infuriated the British lion. The reference by Sir Edmund Monson to some of these charges, in a speech delivered on 6 December 1898, before the British Chamber of Commerce, in Paris, gave some concern to the French Government, and this was the first matter with which M. Cambon had to deal.[1] On 11 December he called M. Delcassé's attention to a speech delivered at Wakefield by the all-powerful Colonial Minister, Joseph Chamberlain, in which the latter, while voicing his hope of seeing friendly relations restored between his own country and France, declared

[1] v. Gooch and Temperley, *British Documents*, 1, No. 237.

that the best way of achieving this object was to state openly what England had on her mind. "There can be no hope of success in the negotiations that are due to be carried on with France unless that Power abandons the vexatious and exasperating policy she has pursued for years. The British Government have no intention of purchasing the friendship of France at the price of concessions for which no compensation is ever forthcoming and the only result of which is to lead to further demands." M. Cambon added that "as regards other Powers than France, M. Chamberlain had none but friendly words, particularly in the case of Germany, "whose interests", he was in the habit of stating, "are in no part of the world irremediably opposed to those of England".

Gone were the days when ambassadors, on leaving Paris to take possession of their posts, were provided with lengthy written instructions. No record has been kept of M. Cambon's conversations with M. Delcassé, before his departure for London. But the almost daily correspondence that ensued between the Minister and his representative in London permits of no doubt whatever as to the intentions of the man who, for a short time, had directed the foreign policy of France. He was determined not only to settle the incident in such a way as to avert all danger of war, but to provide as promptly as possible honourable solutions for all the chief matters at issue between France and England. And of this the British Government were informed, almost at the very moment of M. Cambon's arrival in London, by a despatch from their own Ambassador in Paris.[1] The

[1] "I have heard indirectly, but from a very authoritative source, that M. Cambon is empowered to propose to Your Lordship that all outstanding questions in dispute between France and Great Britain should be dealt with as much as possible simultaneously, and a general agreement

French Government, however, were by no means easy in their minds as regards the intentions of England. They were in receipt of alarming information as to the preparations made by the Admiralty, e.g. the organization in the British Colonies of establishments able to supply munitions, supposing they should be cut off from the home country.[1] Their uneasiness was revealed in M. Delcassé's remarks to Sir Edmund Monson, just after assuring the latter of his desire for peaceful agreement, remarks expressing his astonishment at the continuance of certain measures which, he stated, "lent some semblance of truth to the report that a powerful party, not unrepresented in the Cabinet, was determined on war at any cost". To this the Ambassador replied that England might very well consider her preparations for war as the best means of averting it. Had not M. Delcassé told him, moreover, at the height of the crisis, that in case of a conflict, France would be supported by Russia? Did not this justify the precautionary measures taken on the British side? Whereupon the Minister, to Sir Edmund's amazement, replied that France might furthermore have the support of Germany, whose maritime and commercial interests were becoming more and more opposed to those of England.[2] The Ambassador tactfully brought back the tone of the conversation to a more peaceful level, and in his account of it to Lord Salisbury he put

come to for a comprehensive settlement. I am assured that the President of the Republic and the present Government are honestly anxious to place the relations between the two countries upon the most cordial footing, and I have certainly no reason to believe that this statement is contrary to the truth. It corresponds with all I have heard from M. Delcassé's lips, and especially with what he said in the course of conversation of yesterday." Sir E. Monson to Lord Salisbury, 9 December 1898. Gooch and Temperley, *British Documents*, I, No. 238.

[1] Note from M. Delcassé to the Colonial Minister (minute), 1 December 1898.

[2] Was Mr Chamberlain aware of this conversation before delivering his speech at Wakefield, quoted above?

down M. Delcassé's unexpected outbreak to his Southern temperament and declared himself free from any concern whatever as to the opinion of the overwhelming majority of the French nation. But the mere fact that it was possible for such words to be exchanged almost immediately after the most conciliatory declaration shows conclusively how storm-laden the atmosphere remained.

England was undoubtedly determined to give the impression that she would make no concessions, and that she held herself ready for every emergency. Her representatives abroad had proclaimed the fact to all and sundry. In a letter written several days after the announcement of the French decision to withdraw from Fashoda, Sir Horace Rumbold reported his conversation with Count Goluchowski, who had conveyed to him the impression made in Vienna by what was known there of the warlike preparations of Great Britain. These, Rumbold replied, "were the visible signs of a firm resolve to go to war rather than yield in the difficulty with France". He was personally convinced of the prevalence in England of a strong feeling of irritation, gradually intensified by the scornful tone of certain organs of the Continental Press, which are led " from our unwillingness to resort to the extremity of war, to argue that we must always yield in the end rather than assert ourselves by force of arms."[1]

II

M. Cambon paid his first visit to Lord Salisbury on 9 December, and on the very same day he presented his credentials at Windsor Castle. The Prime Minister was

[1] Sir Horace Rumbold to Lord Salisbury, 9 November 1898. Gooch and Temperley, *British Documents*, I, No. 231.

very courteous in his bearing, but confined his remarks to the International Conference at Rome on the measures to be taken against anarchists. M. Cambon having no instructions on the subject, "the conversation assumed an academic turn. Lord Salisbury then spoke of the Queen, who had expressed her desire to receive the new French Ambassador that very day. He told me I should no doubt find she has aged considerably, but that she is in full possession of her mental faculties and that she attends to the affairs of State just as she did twenty years ago. 'She does not yet hold the record for Royal longevity', he added, 'for that belongs to Louis XIV, but Louis XIV was crowned at the age of five, while the Queen was eighteen when she ascended the throne.' 'There is this difference between Louis XIV and Queen Victoria', I replied, 'that the close of the great King's reign was wrapped in gloom and well did he know the reason, as witness his dying words to his son: "I have loved war too well". Queen Victoria will be spared such gloomy thoughts, for she has always been a lover of peace.' 'Yes, she loves peace', answered the Prime Minister, 'she shrinks with loathing from slaughter in any shape or form.' This was our only allusion to the possibility of a conflict between France and England".

At Windsor, where the Ambassador was given a hearty reception, there was still less chance of an allusion being made to the matter at issue. "I have nothing but praise", writes M. Cambon on 12 December 1898, "for the welcome extended to me by Her Majesty, but I cannot shut my eyes to the fact that while there is on her part, as well as on that of the Prime Minister, a desire to soften the impression caused by the late incidents, feeling in England runs very high and that, when all is said and done, public opinion is the supreme master of the Government."

What M. Cambon had found since his arrival and what led him to believe that the concern felt by his Government was not unfounded, was the rising tide of Imperialistic sentiment in Parliament and in the country. Sir William Harcourt's retirement from the leadership of the Liberal Party attested the disruption with which that Party was threatened under the pressure of new forces. In the Conservative and Liberal Unionist Coalition, Chamberlain, the foremost representative of British Imperialism, was gaining in influence over Lord Salisbury who was growing old. "In spite of his overbearing disposition and his exalted political and social situation", writes M. Cambon on 19 December 1898, "the Prime Minister had to yield: he did so little by little, and without giving way entirely, but he realized that he could not stem the tide of Imperialism, and he allowed himself to drift along with it, while endeavouring to master it as best he could.... There now seems to be no doubt but that if, for some reason or other, the Marquess of Salisbury were to give up the management of affairs, the overwhelming majority of Conservatives and Liberal Unionists would rally under the Imperialist banner. Their union with the Liberals won over to the new conceptions would constitute a body of forceful, restless men, eager for the triumph of the policy of unbridled expansion for the British Empire. Should this development of the rise of a great Imperialist Party come to pass, we could not remain blind to the grave consequences that might result for our country. We should then be confronted, in any affairs we may have to transact with the British Government, with a very different policy from that which for more than eighty years has served as a basis for our dealings with England, a policy which, though inevitably involving occasional friction between neighbouring countries, nevertheless admitted of a sort of general understanding, based on a mutual conviction of the existence of common interests, and on the recognition of mutual rights. With the 'Imperialists' in office, the position would be entirely different: the recent incidents through which we have passed can leave no doubt in our minds as to the determined and uncompromising spirit in which negotiations between the two countries would be conducted on the part of the English, whenever our national interests conflicted, or perhaps merely came into contact with, their own."

M. Cambon dwells at still greater length upon the danger of the situation in his despatch of 22 December.

"I cannot and must not conceal from you", he writes to the Minister, "the general impression that strikes me at every turn since my arrival in London. Superficial as it necessarily is, that impression is but the upshot of my conversations with most of the leading British states-men without distinction of party, but a first impression it remains. It will perhaps be lessened by the individual courtesy and graciousness extended by all and sundry to the Ambassador of the Republic; yet it behoved me to inform you of it.

"The silence, reserve and expectant attitude observed here about the Fashoda affair, and the various matters at issue between France and England, are proof in the first place of a certain scepticism as regards the solution of these problems. It would seem, indeed, that if the Prime Minister entertained the hope of coming to an understanding with us, he would have given some hint of it in the course of the various talks I have already had with him. My attitude, my language were sufficient indication of conciliatory intentions to enable him, had he so desired, to hold out to me some hopeful prospects with regard to his personal dispositions and those of his Government.

"I have had plenty of opportunities to expatiate in his presence on the blessings of peace; his answers were polite, commonplace and uncommittal. So much for the Government and official circles.

"As for the French colony, our countrymen are inclined to take an optimistic view: with them the wish is father to the thought. Such of the English as have business relations with them are of course quite willing to continue, and I am fairly confident that we have not the bulk of the English people against us. But we are up against a certain number of extremely keen politicians. Will they succeed in carrying the nation along with them? That is the whole question.

"Our military and naval attachés are doing their utmost to warn me against optimistic influences. According to them the English are only waiting for the first excuse to pounce upon us, relying on our blunders, on the indiscretions of our Press, on some further incidents in the Colonies: they are ready, and they are satisfied that we are not, and that they will never find a better opportunity....Both these officials, whose experience I cannot ignore, express the same opinion in the plainest and most emphatic terms.

"I should feel less concern at these alarming symptoms if I could perceive some adequate counter-weight to the warlike influences whose unceasing activities are constantly being pointed out to me.

"The Queen, Lord Salisbury and M. Balfour are undoubtedly opposed to war.

"Will Lord Salisbury be strong enough to prevent it? If he had the whole of the Conservative Party behind him, there could be no doubt of this, for he would have the support of the Liberal Party. Unfortunately such is not the case.

"The Conservative Party, while professing the utmost

regard for Lord Salisbury, is not impervious to Mr Chamberlain's propaganda, and as for the Liberal Party, weakened as it has been ever since Mr Gladstone's retirement and death, it is disjointed and crumbling to pieces. It is without a leader, and awaits some sign which it will possibly be given by the prophets of Imperialism.

"Sir William Harcourt and Mr John Morley, of course, are emphatic upholders of peace and desirous to see friendly relations restored with France. They are faithful exponents of Mr Gladstone's ideas, of the older Liberalism with its generous tenets.

"Lord Rosebery and his friends, who are younger and more realistically inclined, seek in an alleged 'National' policy a means of outbidding Mr Chamberlain and they are challenging his popularity.

"Thus political conditions in England—the disruption of the old Parties and their disquieting transformations—all concur in raising serious apprehensions. Our hope is to see Mr Chamberlain and Lord Rosebery at loggerheads, but our fear is to have them join forces against us, and both take their stand on England's alleged grievances against France.

"I am fain to add, moreover, that over here, and particularly for the Prime Minister, who makes no secret of the fact, that political conditions in our own country are too generally the source of what is currently described as 'anxious concern', a feeling which it may be sought to exploit against us.

"We are therefore confronted with a more or less immediate, a more or less contingent, but undeniable danger, and, to use a trite expression, the merest slip may prove fatal."

Naturally enough, this despatch made a deep impression upon M. Delcassé, who hastened to impart it to the French Ambassador at Saint Petersburg. "The concern shown by M. Cambon", he writes to him on 29 December, "calls the more urgently for our attention in that it is supported by the persistent armaments of Great Britain, not only in the United Kingdom, but in every British Colony. In fact, the whole of the information forwarded by the agents of my Deparcment concurs in stressing the importance of the military preparations of England, which, by their very activity, seem to imply the possibility of a conflict."

III

On 11 January 1899, M. Cambon was able to announce to Lord Salisbury the evacuation of Fashoda, reminding him at the same time of the promise given to Baron de Courcel, that, once this first question was out of the way, the British Government would be willing to take up the matter of the necessary territorial delimitation.

"Lord Salisbury admitted having told my predecessor that Fashoda was a 'thorn in the side' of a nature to impede any conversation, but that if and when that issue was settled, it would be possible to talk matters over. He observed that the crux of the matter lay in the fact that, while seeking an outlet for our Ubanghi trade, we attempted to plant our flag in the Nile valley, and that on this point no compromise was possible. He went on to recall Sir Edward Grey's declarations on the subject. I replied that plain speaking was of the utmost necessity, and I added, in my own name, that it would be easy for us to agree upon a line of demarcation which, starting from the South of Tripoli and skirting the Darfur, would cross the Bahr el Ghazal obliquely along the watershed between the Nile and the Ubanghi, and that, without hoisting our flag in the Nile valley, we might obtain for our trade freedom of navigation and a point of embarkation on that river.

"The Prime Minister answered that under those conditions it might be possible to come to an understanding, but that the first thing to be done, in his opinion, was to get some idea of the areas to be delimited and to draw up a map of the country. I reminded him of his suggestion in October last of appointing a Commission of delimitation. He replied that he had merely spoken of Commissions of both countries conducting their investigations separately, and not of a joint French and English delegation. I retorted that while he had indeed spoken of delegates acting separately, their preliminary labours were, according to his own declarations, to have led up to the operations of a joint Commission. I added that in any case we ought to agree on the principle of such delimitation, so as to give a lead to our delegates. In conclusion, Lord Salisbury asked for time to think it over."

After thus sketching out an acceptable solution of the most urgent matter at issue, M. Cambon boldly tackled the whole problem of Franco-British relations:

"I observed to him", he writes, "that it was important to put an end to the strained relations between our two countries, that if the British Government had anything on their minds, I begged him to tell me so and that I was quite willing to enter upon a frank explanation upon all the differences of which the Press makes so much ado, and which struck me as imaginary. Lord Salisbury at once alluded to the feeling caused by the measures adopted in Madagascar against British interests.

"I replied that no sooner had formal complaint been made to us concerning certain measures taken by the military authorities on the spot, without the knowledge of our Government, than these measures were repealed; that the economic system of the island could not be altered in a day, and that the trend of public opinion in France would very much depend upon the way in which the alteration was asked for. I thereupon mentioned the bad effect produced by the publication of the last Blue Book.

"'People seem to forget', he retorted with unusual animation, 'that Parliament meets three weeks hence and that I must needs defend myself.' 'I know that', was my rejoinder, 'but I consider that if in Parliament Madagascar affairs are raised in a very friendly tone, a current opinion which is beginning to set in, in France, against the abuses of protectionism is bound to become more pronounced, and that our Government will be able to consider the possibility of a reform, but with hasty words nothing can be accomplished.'

"I then explained to him, still speaking in my own name, the state of French public opinion in the economic sphere.

"He listened to my explanations with interest, and he answered that in Parliament these matters would no longer be dealt with by irresponsible journalists, but by responsible men, used to weighing their words.

"Upon which, his interest seeming to flag, he went on to observe: 'I have nothing to say to you about Newfoundland, a bone of contention between us for the last sixty years. Now, the Newfoundlanders themselves have taken up the matter. It has developed into a triangular duel, and may last for a long time yet'.

"Such is the substance of our conversation, which I did my best to render as cordial as possible. If our Press could manage to let English affairs lie dormant for a while, and cease to supply English journalists with excuses for polemics, I believe it would soon be possible to enter into negotiations."

It is interesting to compare this conversation, as reported by M. Cambon, with the account given of it by Lord Salisbury to the British Ambassador in Paris. The Prime Minister's impression is just what M. Cambon wished it to be. He (Lord Salisbury) found his (M. Cambon's) manner exceedingly conciliatory and his language obviously chosen so as to avoid " any suggestion that might be distasteful to Her Majesty's Government ". While duly noting M. Cambon's insistence on the fact that he spoke in his own name, and reserving his right to consult General Kitchener and Lord Cromer as to the question of delimitation east of Lake Chad, he had recognized that the Ambassador's observations, "if I rightly understood them, indicated the elements of a settlement at which both countries might arrive without sacrificing their own essential interests ".[1]

And as it actually proved, it was on the basis laid in the course of this conversation that a settlement of the Fashoda issue was arrived at on 21 March following. It also foreshadowed the wider negotiation which, five years later, and in spite of many severe hitches, at last culminated in a general agreement on the matters remaining at issue between the two countries.

Meanwhile, the goal plainly pointed to by M. Cambon was still distant. During the next few months, certain minor affairs—e.g. the extension of the French concession at Shanghai; the establishment of a coaling station at Muscat—renewed the mutual irritation. On 13 August 1899, after receiving Sir Edmund Monson, who had come to take leave of him before starting on a tour in the Vosges mountains, he writes to M. Paul Cambon:

"I took advantage of this opportunity to have a frank explanation with him on the subject of our relations with England. I reminded him—a fact he admitted— that in accordance with my public declarations, I had

---

[1] Lord Salisbury to Sir Edmund Monson, 11 January 1899, Gooch and Temperley, *British Documents*, 1, No. 240.

consistently endeavoured to practise a policy of mutual understanding, which I consider to be of equal benefit to both countries; that to represent that policy in London, I had chosen a man not only remarkable for his eminent qualities, but sharing my conviction to the full. 'Well', I added, 'I am bound to observe that while Her Majesty's Government, as we are fain to believe, nourish the same friendly sentiments as we do, those sentiments have not availed to bring about a solution of minor affairs, which, one would think, ought to be very soon settled with a little active good will.'

" . . . Lastly, reading out to him a few passages of your despatch—in a private and personal way—I asked him if he was not struck by these signs of a good will which was beginning to lose heart, and whether he did not think it time to prevent the idea from becoming general that there is no possibility of coming to an understanding with England."

It took equal courage, patience, and statesmanship to bury old quarrels and bring about first of all the compromise of 1899, and then, in spite of dangerous crosscurrents, the understanding of 1904.

11. The part played in International Relations by the Conversations between the General Staffs on the Eve of the World War

by

PIERRE RENOUVIN

THE study of international relations during the period preceding the World War has revealed the importance of the part played by the General Staffs, whether on account of the influence exerted on certain occasions by their war plans on the guidance of foreign policy, or through the contribution made to diplomatic arrangements by military or naval conversations and technical conventions. These matters, however, have not yet been made the subject of critical study.

We are aware, of course, of the importance that conversations between General Staffs may assume in defining or interpreting the obligations imposed by an alliance; it was by a military protocol that the Franco-Russian Convention of 1892 was amended in 1900 to cover the contingency of an English, and not merely of a German aggression; it was also by an agreement between the respective Staffs that Art. 2 of that Franco-Russian Convention was interpreted, in 1911, in a sense restricting the obligations devolving upon France. The importance of the letters exchanged between General Conrad von Hoetzendorff and General von Moltke, in January 1909, also gave rise to interesting discussions. Specific examples, moreover, point to the vital part that may be played by a plan of campaign at the most crucial moments; it was the German General Staff which, on

1 August 1914, proclaimed itself unable to direct its concentration against Russia alone, because it had always prepared for "war on both fronts"; it was the Russian General Staff which, on 31 July 1914, led the Government to decree general mobilization, because partial mobilization would put the whole mechanism out of order; it was the Austro-Hungarian General Staff which adopted a plan of concentration of such a nature that, five days after mobilizing against Servia, it was obliged to "clear up" the attitude of Russia. Governments are bound by such technical considerations as these, which they have been unable to foresee or to control. The following, therefore, is a problem of exceptional importance: to what extent have the international activities of the General Staffs been guided or controlled by the Governments? That problem I cannot attempt to study in detail. My object is merely to supply an example, and to inquire into the relations between the British and French General Staffs from 1905 to 1914, for the purpose of ascertaining the part played by such technical arrangements in the political relations between the two countries.

I

What were the different stages—as far as it is now possible to ascertain with the help of available records and evidence—in these relations between the British and French General Staffs?

(a) From a *military* point of view, the first conversation of which we find a trace in the British and French records was held at the close of December 1905. The French military attaché in London, Colonel Huguet, meets General Grierson, Director of Military Operations, at the War Office. At a time when the impending meeting of the Algeciras Conference threatens to raise further Franco-German difficulties, the French General Staff endeavours to ascertain whether support would be forthcoming from England in case of war. General Grierson's reply is to the effect that the hypothesis of British intervention on the Continent has been considered by the War Office.[1] It is a "private" conversation, "as between friends", which in no way prejudges any decisions by the Government.

On 31 December 1905, the permanent secretary of the Committee of Imperial Defence, Sir George Clarke, writes down a few questions which are communicated to the French General Staff through the medium of a writer, Colonel Repington: "Have the French Military Authorities considered the question of Franco-British co-operation in case of a Franco-German war?" Can it be assumed that France "will not violate Belgian neutrality, unless compelled to do so by a previous violation on the part of the German armies"? "What plan of campaign is suggested?" The French reply on the first point is plain: what is required is "to bring over all available British troops", as promptly as possible, to the left of the French Army; on the second point, it is in the affirmative; on the third it is non-committal: it is difficult to draw up a plan of co-operation beforehand; it is better to be content with contemplating a common action "to be decided upon according to circumstances". The War Office thereupon puts the finishing touches to the organization of an expeditionary force.

In October 1906, General Ewart superseded General Grierson. He considered it necessary to "revise" the arrangements for the formation and transportation of the expeditionary force, because the British Army is being reorganized and because, on the other hand, the plan for the mobilization and concentration of the

---

[1] Gooch and Temperley, *British Documents*, III, No. 211.

French Armies has been amended. He therefore drafted a new scheme, which he completes in July 1907. Before communicating it to the French military attaché, the General Staff advise the Foreign Office of its intention, while specifying that this document is no more binding than the last on the British Government. Sir Edward Grey signified his approval.[1]

As from 1910, General Sir Henry Wilson succeeds General Ewart. In spite of the fact that some little time before, the Committee of Imperial Defence had expressed some doubts as to the advisability of sending over an expeditionary force to France—instead of holding it in reserve with a view to direct intervention in Belgium— the bases of Franco-British military co-operation remain. Further exchanges of views define with greater precision the particulars of the possible intervention: the expeditionary force is to comprise the whole of the Army mobilized—six Divisions; the mobilization is speeded up to such a degree that no later than the twelfth day of the British mobilization, all these troops shall have completed their landing in France; the place of landing, which was originally to have been Boulogne, is moved back to Havre; lastly, the British forces are to complete their concentration in the region of Maubeuge. On 20 July 1911—at the height of the Agadir crisis—these results are embodied in a report signed in Paris by General Wilson and by General Dubail.[2] Thenceforward the technical study of all details relating to the transportation, halting-places and victualling of the British forces are pushed on actively. These studies, however, do not seem to assume a wider scope: we have no documents showing conclusively that the conceptions of

---

[1] Gooch and Temperley, *British Documents*, iii, No. 221 b.

[2] *Les Armées françaises dans la Grande Guerre*, i, 49; also in Gooch and Temperley, *ibid.* vii, No. 640.

the French General Staff concerning the operations as a whole were communicated to the War Office, either officially or semi-officially. The only point giving rise to an exchange of views is the question of Belgian neutrality. On 26 November 1912, General Sir Henry Wilson, in a conversation with General de Castelnau,[1] warns the French General Staff not to yield to the temptation it might—and did—feel at one time—to conduct a preventive offensive through French territory.

(b) From the *naval* point of view, the progress of the conversations is somewhat similar, but slower. On 2 January 1906, the First Sea Lord, Sir John Fisher, in a conversation with the French naval attaché, Captain Mercier de Lostende, describes the part that would be played by the British squadrons in case of a Franco-German war. Was this conversation the earliest? M. Élie Halévy[2] is inclined to think that the British Admiralty must previously have been in contact with some high French personage. All that can be said on the point is that this previous conversation, if held at all, has left no trace. Moreover, the exchange of views in 1906 would not appear to have resulted in a definite plan of co-operation between the naval authorities of the two countries.

At the end of 1908, when a further international crisis —that of Bosnia and Herzegovina—confronts the world with the possibility of a European conflict, conversations are resumed, and this time their object is to define the respective parts to be played by the two Navies and their zones of action. But this exchange of views, known to us only by a later document, has left no trace in writing. The same is the case in August 1911, at the time of the Agadir crisis; the questions examined—apportionment

[1] The fact is recorded in the *Mémoires du Maréchal Joffre*, i, 125–6; cf. also the exact text of the British communication in *Documents diplomatiques français*, 3ème série, T. v, No. 53, footnote.

[2] *Histoire du peuple anglais au XIXème siècle*, Épilogue ii, p. 181.

of squadrons and commands; organization of the defence of the Straits of Dover—merely result in a "verbal agreement".[1]

Not before the spring of 1912 do the conversations take on a more definite turn. When the failure of the Haldane mission to Berlin and the further increase of the German naval forces in the North Sea lead the British Government to alter the distribution of the British squadrons, and to bring nearer home part of the ships previously assigned to the defence of the Mediterranean, the British Admiralty feels the need of setting up a more definite agreement with the French Navy. "The time has come", says Mr Winston Churchill to the French naval attaché (17 July 1912), "for the Staffs to talk matters over and to reach some sort of a Convention."[2] At the beginning of July, a draft agreement was drawn up in London, which, after being discussed and amended several times, finally took shape in February 1913. At the beginning of April 1913, the French naval attaché in London was able to report that the Admiralty considers "the agreement" as "definitely concluded"; the reference is to three documents laying the foundations of Franco-British naval co-operation in the Mediterranean, the Western Channel and the Straits of Dover.[3] Concurrently, a similar co-operation is provided for in the Far East.[4]

The above particulars are very likely incomplete, but they are sufficient, I think, for the understanding of the general trend of these technical conversations, for the appreciation of the character, and the definition of their

[1] *Doc. dipl. français*, 3ème série, T. II, No. 336, footnote.
[2] *Doc. dipl. français*, 3ème série, T. II, No. 332; T. III, No. 50, 189, 207, 420, 446; T. IV, No. 15, 398.
[3] The text of these agreements is given in *Doc. dipl. français*, 3ème série, T. V, No. 397 (14 February 1913).
[4] *Doc. dipl. français*, 3ème série, T. V, No. 203; T. VI, No. 198.

results. Until the autumn of 1912, both from the military and the naval points of view, the conversations are intermittent: at all times of international strain, the General Staffs consult together; when the danger was over, the exchanges of views became less frequent, or ended altogether. Only after the well-known exchange of letters of 21–22 November 1913 does their co-operation become permanent. For the land forces, this exchange results in a whole series of technical arrangements which are not collected in a single text, and do not represent a previous understanding in respect of the plan of operations; as for the naval forces, the joint arrangements arrived at were given the shape of conventions.

II

What is the part taken in this matter by the governments? This is the point I would now consider. It presents two different angles:

I. To what extent did the General Staffs act on their own initiative? Did they ·negotiate "on their own account" or on that of their governments?

II. To what extent did the governments approve of the technical arrangements thus worked out by the General Staffs?

I. Seemingly, the initiative belongs entirely to the General Staffs. But as a matter of fact, what is the position?

On the French side, there is no doubt but that the conversations between the General Staffs were not only authorized, but desired by the government. It was the Prime Minister Rouvier who in January 1905 confidentially informed Ambassador Paul Cambon of his desire to see them entered upon. In 1911, it was on the initiative of the Quai d'Orsay itself that the French naval attaché in London approached the Admiralty. The

General Staff reported to the Prime Minister (February 1912) and to the President of the Republic (March 1912) the results obtained in the course of the previous conversations. In October 1912 it was the Prime Minister, M. Poincaré, who issued instructions for the turn to be imparted to the pourparlers, the upshot of which was the Naval Agreement of 1913.

On the British side, the highest authorities in the state were likewise cognizant, from the first, of the object of these conversations between the General Staffs. As early as 20 December 1905, during a royal audience, the French Ambassador, Paul Cambon, made a tentative allusion to the intention the British Government might have of sending over an expeditionary force to the Continent, in case of a Franco-German war. King Edward advised the Ambassador to broach the matter with the Secretary of State for Foreign Affairs. Sir Edward Grey expressly authorized the earliest exchange of views in January 1906; he agreed to the holding of "non-official" conversations between the Admiralty and the War Office, on the one hand; and the French military and naval authorities on the other. He merely seemed to be somewhat mistrustful of the manner in which the conversations had been started, and to regret the part played by Colonel Repington on this occasion. "...I did not go so far as to disapprove of communications by intermediaries", he jots down on 13 January 1906. "I reserved my opinion, because I did not know what they were. I do, however, approve of their being continued in a proper manner, i.e. with the cognizance of the official heads of the Admiralty and War Office."[1] The one and only reserve he formulates applies therefore to the choice of the original intermediary. General Grier-

[1] Gooch and Temperley, *British Documents*, III, No. 212, *vide* also pp. 169–70.

son, Director of Military Operations at the War Office, and Lord Tweedmouth, First Sea Lord, were then given a written authorization to conduct the conversations. In July 1907, when the Lyttelton Memorandum was submitted to him, Sir Edward Grey again grants an explicit authorization. In 1908 and 1909 the Committee of Imperial Defence were kept informed of the technical negotiations.

On both sides, therefore, the technical negotiations were expressly authorized, and not merely tolerated by the governments. It is of course true that in England, the government's approval was given by the Prime Minister and the Secretary of State for Foreign Affairs, not by the Cabinet as a whole; and it may be that the same was the case on the French side—a point it is difficult to make sure of in the present state of our information. Be this as it may, we may safely conclude that the initiative of the General Staffs, approved of and supervised by the authorities responsible for the general policy to be followed, was more apparent than real.

II. In both cases, moreover, these technical arrangements by no means imply a promise of intervention. From the very first, Sir Edward Grey was careful to specify that the conversations between the General Staffs could only be of a provisional and non-committal character. He declared to M. Paul Cambon that they would "be binding upon" neither government (15 January 1906).

At each stage of the exchanges of views between the soldiers, the participants never fail to recall the principle adopted from the first. In the memorandum he forwards to the Foreign Office and to the French military attaché on 26 July 1907, Chief of Staff General Lyttelton writes as follows: "This paper is to be·regarded merely as the expression of the views of the British General Staff on what might be done under certain circumstances, but is in no way binding on the government". In a letter dated 24 March 1911, in which he takes note of the modifications adopted as regards the eventual transportation of the British expeditionary force, Colonel Huguet specifies that this plan "is in no way binding upon the British Government, who remain free to intervene or not", free also "themselves to decide upon the strength of that Force". When General Sir Henry Wilson comes over to Paris, on 20 July 1911, to confer with General Dubail, he has an express declaration put down on the agenda: "...The pourparlers entered upon can in no way be binding upon the British and French Governments". The conversations between the Naval General Staffs are subject to the same reserve. The technical agreements concluded in the spring of 1913 all begin by recalling this vital point: "In the event of a war in which Great Britain and France are allied against the Triple Alliance", runs the text entitled "Joint action in the Mediterranean" (10 February 1913); "in the event of being allied with the French Government in a war with Germany," runs the arrangement relating to the "Defence of Dover Straits" (23 January 1913).[1]

Lastly, in the letters exchanged between the British and the French Governments, the same declaration is expressly formulated: "From time to time in recent years", writes Sir Edward Grey, "the French and British naval and military experts have consulted together. It has always been understood that such consultation does not restrict the freedom of either Government to decide, at any future time, whether or not to assist the other with armed force. We have agreed that consultation between experts is not—and ought not to be—

[1] *Doc. dipl. français*, 3ème série, T. v, No. 397; cp. Gooch and Temperley, *British Documents*, vii, No. 640; xi, No. 319.

regarded as an engagement that commits either Government to action...".[1]

"Legally" speaking, the position was therefore as follows: the British and French General Staffs had jointly defined the conditions of the collaboration they might extend to each other in the event of a European war; the Governments, on the contrary, have contracted no obligation. The sole object of the technical military and naval arrangements is to give immediate efficacy to a British intervention, should it eventually be decided upon. On both sides the General Staffs are thus enabled at once to apply the measures agreed upon, instead of having to improvise them. Is that a negligible result? Certainly not, considering the situation that will occur at the beginning of a war: in the eyes of the French General Staff it is vital that the British expeditionary force should take up its position on the extreme left of the French line before the first battles; it is no less imperative that from the very first day of the mobilization the French Mediterranean Squadron shall be free to devote the major part of its forces to convoying the troops that are to be brought home from North Africa, and that it shall consequently be cognizant of the part assigned to the British naval units, without it being necessary to proceed to an exchange of views. The arrangements entered into by the General Staffs therefore make for a saving of time and dispense with the necessity of tentative measures. Seeing that it is to Germany's interest to deliver a sudden attack, it behoves her possible future adversaries to take the necessary measures to thwart her plans.

Now does not the mere existence of these arrangements between the General Staffs impart to Franco-

[1] See note on previous page.

British relations a particularly intimate character, notwithstanding the reserves expressly formulated? It undeniably does. At every critical juncture in international relations—in January 1906, at the beginning of 1909, in the summer of 1911—the exchange of views to which the General Staffs proceed implies that the idea of a possible intervention is admitted by British official circles. Nay, the provisions of these technical agreements have the value, as it were, of a moral obligation. On the military side the British General Staff advises the French General Staff to undertake not to advance into Belgian territory previous to a violation of neutrality on the part of Germany; it agrees, on the other hand, to the suggestion that, instead of attempting a direct defence of Belgian neutrality by means of a landing at Antwerp, the British expeditionary force shall act in co-operation with the French Armies. Between these two results of the conversations there is, in principle, no *immediate relation.* But the French General Staff is justified in assuming that the collaboration of the British forces is the consideration agreed to for the promise it has given. On the naval side, the result of the technical arrangements is to concentrate the bulk of the French forces in the Mediterranean, and in consequence to leave the shores of the Channel and the North Sea practically open, under the protection of the British fleet; were Great Britain, after wishing for these arrangements, to allow the German fleet to cross the Dover Straits, she would be exposing France to danger and give the impression of a breach of faith. "Are you going to let Cherbourg and Brest be bombarded", M. Paul Cambon inquires of Sir Edward Grey, on 1 August 1914, "when it is by your advice and with your consent, and to serve your interests as well as our own, that we have concentrated all our ships far away?" The existence of this "moral bond" is one of the arguments put forward by Sir Eyre Crowe on 31 July 1914 in his note to Sir Edward Grey.[1] Accordingly M. Halévy (p. 183) makes bold to assert that this understanding "practically amounts to an alliance". For my part, I would not go so far. Whatever may be the value—when the time comes—of this argument based on a "moral obligation", the fact remains, none the less, that the British Government had made no promise to France: they intend to remain masters of their decision. They claim full liberty to intervene, or not to intervene (Halévy, p. 600). That liberty is perhaps no longer so entire as they are pleased to declare, and as they possibly believe it to be. But the uncertainty they allow to remain as regards their intentions serves the designs of their general policy: if France were to have in her hands a formal undertaking—i.e. a treaty of alliance —if under given circumstances she could confidently rely upon British intervention, who knows but that she would adopt a more determined attitude towards Germany? The doubt that remains as to a possible British intervention compels the French to act cautiously, to abstain, in the event of a crisis, from any hazardous move. By reserving, down to the last minute, the right to fulfil or not to fulfil the hopes she has raised, Great Britain keeps in hand a means of pressure on France. This design, of course, is not expressed formally; it may possibly be unconscious; none the less it would appear to account for the policy of the Foreign Office towards France between 1906 and 1914.

On the French side, at all events, in spite of the repeated assurances given to their colleagues by the British naval and military officers, in spite of the "affectionate trust" that prevails between the representatives of the General Staffs, the Army chiefs remain

[1] Gooch and Temperley, *British Documents*, xi, No. 369.

uneasy as regards, not so much the fact of British intervention, as the actual date at which it would come about. When in France the order of mobilization is issued in the event of a conflict with Germany, it will be necessary to wait for the British Government to come to a decision before carrying out the technical Franco-British arrangements. The first day of the British mobilization will therefore be subsequent to the first day of the French mobilization. What will be the importance of this delay? The question is a vital one: if the British order of mobilization is too long in coming, it will not be possible to concentrate the expeditionary force in time to take part in the first great battle on French soil. This it is that gives concern to the French General Staff. "The first decision", writes the French military attaché, on 10 September 1911, "will be the hardest to obtain. If France, in her conflict with Germany, does not exhaust every means of conciliation, public opinion, in England, will be divided, and the military intervention of Great Britain may be considerably delayed." Furthermore, will the British Government be willing to send over their expeditionary force, before they are certain a German naval attack is out of the question? "It may be assumed", writes one of the chief Army leaders, "that the mobilization will not be carried out immediately, for Great Britain will be unwilling to commence operations on the Continent before fighting a 'naval battle'." Accordingly, in the "Bases du Plan XVII" submitted to the Higher War Council on 18 April 1913, General Joffre expresses the opinion that British support remains doubtful. "We shall therefore be doing wisely in not taking the British forces into account in our plans of operation."[1]

The British military authorities are conscious of this

[1] *Les Armées françaises*, I, 19.

disadvantage: "they are thinking", writes Colonel Huguet,[1] "of proceeding with the first measures of mobilization", without awaiting the decision of their Government. How far they actually contemplated this plan is a secret which neither the documents nor the evidence available have hitherto disclosed to us.

The above particulars are not meant to solve the complex problems raised by the relations between the General Staffs on the eve of the World War; their chief object is to draw attention to these problems, which the historians have but very rarely approached. The field is one in which diplomatic action and the activities of the military and naval technicians meet and complete each other. The study is all the more difficult in that it would be necessary, for the purpose of appreciating the exact value of the facts, to be able to investigate the practical operation of the governmental mechanism and to determine, above all, to what extent the governments then controlled the activities of the General Staffs. It must be recognized that historical research on these subjects is by no means easy for the present: the soldiers are even more secretive than the diplomatists. Even if and when it becomes possible, in every country, to have access to the official records, we are very unlikely to find in them a complete picture of the facts. Does not the experience· of the Franco-British conversations, from 1906 to 1914, show that many of the conversations between the General Staffs have not been recorded in protocols? It is therefore with a confession of weakness that I must conclude. And this confession will hardly come as a surprise to you.

[1] *Les Armées françaises*, I, 75.

INDEX

INDEX

INDEX